The Unschool Challenge

Sue Elvis

Sue Elvis

P.O. Box 57, Hill Top

NSW, 2575

Australia

First published © 2023 Sue Elvis

ISBN: 978-0-6454867-2-8

For my sister Vicky with love

Contents

Welcome to the Unschool Challenge

I'm so excited you're here, and I can't wait for you to try out my unschooling challenges. But first, I'd like to share some introductory information.

The Challenges

What is a challenge? It could be a problem, an obstacle, a concern: something we need to conquer if we want to move forward.

A challenge can also be a task. When we accept a challenge, we know we'll probably work hard, but we also know there will be something good at the end. We'll have gained something from the experience. It will have changed us in some way.

In this book, you'll find lots of challenges or tasks that will help remove the challenges or concerns that might prevent you from living an unschooling life with your family.

My unschooling challenges are designed to overcome the challenges of unschooling!

The challenges illustrate the unschooling principles and will give you a better understanding of them. Despite the often fearsome reputation of challenges, you won't find the ones I've written difficult to do. They come with step-by-step suggestions and lots of questions that will point you in the right direction. All you will need to provide is a willingness to ponder and explore and an openness to changing your thinking if required.

Who Are the Challenges For?

If you have doubts about unschooling - does it make sense, or are the critics right? - the challenges will help.

Or if you're saying, "We want to unschool, but we don't know how to incorporate its principles into our lives," this book will give you many ideas for things to do. I have stuffed it with practical suggestions.

If you feel stuck and life has lost its sparkle, these challenges might reignite your passion for unschooling.

The challenges will give you record-keeping tips that might allow you to unschool while fulfilling any homeschooling requirements.

I hope my book of challenges demolishes all your concerns - whatever they are - so you're free to love unconditionally, trust, and live a full unschooling life bursting with learning with your kids.

Extra Challenges

Some challenges have additional ideas that you could explore.

Stories

I've added a story or two to each challenge to illustrate the ideas contained within them. I'm grateful my husband Andy and our children don't mind me sharing our experiences. They are very generous people!

If you don't know my family, Andy and I have eight children. Felicity was born in 1987, and Gemma-Rose joined us in 2004. Duncan, Callum, Imogen, Charlotte, Thomas, and Sophie come somewhere in between.

We live in Australia and are long-time unschoolers: my kids never went to school. I have over 28 years of homeschool registration experience and picked up many tips for fulfilling the requirements of our state of NSW without compromising our unschooling way of life.

There are a few short stories for my Christian unschooling friends among the many that will appeal to everyone.

Related Reading

I have added some related reading suggestions to most challenges. These stories come from my first two unschooling books, *Curious Unschoolers* and *Radical Unschool Love*. If you haven't already read them, I hope you'll check them out!

A Challenges Notebook

You might like to keep a challenges notebook.

Every time you do a challenge, you could jot down the following:

- Answers to any questions you pondered.

- What you and your kids did during the challenge.

- The outcome of the challenge.

- How you felt.

- What you learnt.

- Any changes you'd like to make.

- And any other relevant thoughts and information.

Writing things down often seems like too much trouble, doesn't it? We might be tempted to read, think briefly and move on. But writing helps us sort out our thoughts and feelings, so we get to the heart of the issue. Sometimes it takes us to unexpected places. It's helpful.

When we reread our written words a year or even a month or two later, we often realise how far we've travelled. Our ideas might have changed a lot!

And having our thoughts and ideas in writing can encourage us when we're having a wobbly moment. We might reread what we've written, remember what we're trying to achieve and then step forward with renewed resolution and enthusiasm.

Keeping a notebook will ensure you get the most out of this book, so I hope you'll take the time to write about each challenge.

How to Use This Book

You could start at the beginning and work your way to the end. Or you might like to dip into the challenges randomly. You could choose one that appeals to you or answers a current need. That's the approach I'd take!

You might like to focus on one challenge at a time. Go slowly and extract all you can from one before moving forward to the next. There's no hurry.

Of course, you can do each challenge more than once. Wouldn't it be interesting to see if the results of a challenge change over time?!

So that's the introduction. Now it's time for the challenges!

The Challenges

1: Write Your Pixar Story

Austin Kleon wrote in his book, *Show Your Work* that if we want to share our work with the world, we need to tell great stories. He mentioned the Pixar Story Structure:

Once upon a time, there was ____. Every day, ____. One day ____. Because of that, ____. Because of that, ____. Until finally ____.

I decided to challenge myself to write a Pixar story about my life.

Once upon a time, there was a mother who had lots of children of different ages that she was homeschooling. This mother's heart overflowed with love for her kids. She wanted to give them the best.

Every day, the mother planned things for her older children to learn about. Unfortunately, they weren't interested. "Why do we have to do this?" they asked. "Because I said so!" replied the mother, who didn't have time to think of a better answer because the baby was crying and the toddler was complaining. (They were hungry.)

Every day, the mother forced her older kids to learn what she thought was important while caring for her younger ones. It was hard work. There were battles.

Every day, the pressure inside the mother built up until she exploded into a dragon mother.

One day, when the dragon mother threatened to appear, the real mother ran outside. She sat on the garden wall in the sun, breathing deeply, trying to calm down. After a while, she noticed her kids peering anxiously through the window at her. Were they afraid of what she was going to do next?

Because of those looks, the mother decided that things had to change. She raced inside and said, "Make a picnic. We're going bushwalking!"

Because of that picnic, the mother and kids enjoyed their day. They rediscovered what was important. It wasn't other people's expectations; it wasn't work no one was interested in; it was each other. The mother listened to her kids instead of the outside voices and rejected everything that wasn't working.

Until finally, life was good. It was peaceful, and everyone was happy. They were all learning. The family had found their way to unschooling.

The Challenge

Write your Pixar story. You might have more than one of them. Your story may illustrate how and why your family arrived at unschooling.

Of course, you might not yet have adopted this way of life. Maybe you still a bit unsure about unschooling.

Or you may agree with the principles of unschooling but don't know how to put them into action.

After reading *The Unschool Challenge*, I hope all that will change, and your unschooling Pixar story will end with the words:

Because of *The Unschool Challenge*, I learnt more about the principles of unschooling. I tried them out, got excited and felt encouraged and brave. I no longer hung back. One by one, I put the principles into action.

Until finally, life was good. It was peaceful, and everyone was happy and learning. My family had found their way to unschooling.

If that happens, I'll grin!

2: Prepare for a New Unschooling Year

We all know learning doesn't just happen during the official school hours. Kids can learn anytime, including weekends and the long summer holidays. So can we. We don't really need to artificially split up a year into terms and holidays or a day into school hours and free time. Every day of the year could look exactly the same. But, when my kids were registered unschooling homeschoolers, that didn't actually happen.

Our unschooling year had seasons, ebbing and flowing, changing naturally as we moved from the hope and anticipation we felt as we hung an empty calendar on the wall on the first day of January to the excitement of Christmas almost twelve months later.

Throughout the year, we adjusted our days, taking into account what was going on in our lives. The seasons and the weather affected what we did. And so did our health and our levels of energy. The needs of each member of our family also influenced our days. When we had babies and toddlers, they always came first. And so did the various crises that came our way.

Outside activities and music lessons that were only offered during the school terms also contributed to the look of our days. And then there was my husband's work. Andy is a school teacher, so, for us, the school holidays were times for relaxing, slow mornings, late nights, and setting off on family outings while he was home. I also forgot about homeschool record-keeping for a few weeks. I could stop watching out for educational experiences to write about in our records book and take a break from strewing.

When Gemma-Rose had just turned nine and Sophie was several years older, I wrote about the start of a new unschooling year:

Andy returns to work tomorrow. He's a primary school teacher.

"This is Dad's last day of holiday," I say to the girls.

They are quiet for a moment, and then, it suddenly dawns on them. "You mean the new school term starts tomorrow?" says Sophie, a smile appearing on her face.

I nod, and Gemma-Rose shouts, "Hooray! You can read to us again."

"Well…" I begin. "I didn't say *our* term begins tomorrow." The smiles disappear.

"But there's so much we want to do," says Sophie.

"You don't have to wait for me," I say. "You're good at learning things by yourselves."

"I know, but what about reading? We like you reading to us, and everything's much more fun when we do things together."

Sophie presents me with a list:

Things I want to do

* Watch *Space Odyssey, Voyage to the Planets*. Read the book, too and play around on the website.

* Learn all about planets and space.

* Read *A Little Bush Maid*.

* Learn about New Zealand.

* Learn about the Second World War.

* Learn about Australian birds.

* Watch more Gilbert and Sullivan musicals.

* Learn poetry.

* Read *Little Women*.

* Learn more about maths.

* Learn about water.

* Learn to play the organ.

It looks like my lazy summer days are over. I need to think about how I can help my girls learn all they want to know. Maybe I should walk around the house looking for appropriate resources to strew.

I love Sophie's and Gemma-Rose's enthusiasm and impatience to acquire more knowledge. After a long relaxing summer, they can't wait until we return to our usual school term rhythm.

As a child, I also looked forward to the start of the new school year. I was eager to wear my new uniform, meet up again with my friends, and find out who my new teacher was. A few days later, all that enthusiasm would seep away. It was business as usual as we headed back to the grind. I tried looking ahead to the next summer holiday, but all I could see was tedious work, week after week. I sighed.

I can also remember, years ago, sighing as a homeschooling mother. I'd start the year with great anticipation, armed with new resources and ideas, and then, a few weeks into the term, my enthusiasm would die. Teaching my children no longer seemed like an exciting adventure. It was just one long hard struggle. But that was in the days when we weren't unschooling.

My girls won't be sighing in a few days or even a few weeks. I'm sure they'll still be bouncing around, full of the joy of learning. Their enthusiasm won't disappear, and mine won't either. And I am very grateful for that. I'm glad we found our way to unschooling.

Sophie appears again, a book in her hand. "This looks interesting," she says. "Perhaps I can add this to my list of things I want to do."

I read the title: *Aircraft of Australia and New Zealand.* "Aviation: Amelia Earhart, Charles Kingsford Smith, The Wright Brothers." I pause as I try to remember more.

"Can you spell those names?" asks Sophie. "I'll go and look them up."

The new unschooling year has begun.

Perhaps you're at the start of a new unschooling year. You've taken down your tree and packed away the Christmas decorations, and now you and your children are eager to dive deeper into your interests. You may be looking forward to moving naturally from the celebration season to a new learning phase.

But how will you use all those empty days ahead? What will you do, and where will you go? Do you have hopes and dreams? Where will you start?

You could begin your year by taking up this challenge!

The Challenge

1. Write a list of things you hope to do.

Perhaps there's a hobby you've always wanted to try. Or you've dreamed of writing a book. Would you like to learn a second language? Ride a bike or a horse? Go for long hikes? Investigate new recipes? How about saying yes more often? Become a better listener? Do you want to be more adventurous this year: try new things and ponder new ideas.

2. Write a list of what your kids would like to do.

Have some family conversations where everyone shares their ideas for the year. Also, chat with your kids during one-on-one times. Would they like to go camping? Or do they dream of having a pet? Are your older children ready to learn to drive? (That's a scary one!) What about creating a YouTube channel? There may be smaller things they'd like to do, such as listen to read-alouds or go on more outings. How about dedicating a day each week for adventures?

This challenge is not about writing a homeschooling plan you expect your kids to follow. It's more about identifying the things everyone would like to do and then working out how you will do them.

The Challenge 'Rules'

1. You can put whatever you like on your own lists, but you can't put things on your kids' lists. For example, you can only add 'write more stories' or 'practise spelling' to their lists if that's what they'd really like to do!

2. You have to seriously consider all of your kids' ideas and be prepared to help put them into action. Will you need to be brave? Will you need to step outside your comfort zone? Will you need to join in?

If the ideas seem impossible, examine them from all angles instead of rejecting them. Get your kids' input. Can the ideas be modified and still satisfy everyone?

3. Give your kids and yourself permission to change your minds about anything on the lists. If you start a language course but then decide it's not for you, drop it and try something else.

4. You can add items to your lists as the year progresses.

5. And if no one has any ideas, you could strew a few!

Of course, you can take up this challenge before the beginning of a new year. You could also do it at the start of a new season, or any time you feel in a rut and want to reignite your family's passion for learning.

Related Reading

The Changing Seasons of the Unschooling Year: Curious Unschoolers

An Unschooling Holiday: Curious Unschoolers

Funny How Things Change: Curious Unschoolers

3: Evaluate Unschooling

When we started homeschooling, I had one big hope: I wanted my kids to love learning. I'd lost my curiosity at school and didn't want this to happen to my children. I dreamed of spending long days doing exciting things with kids who were interested in everything.

I also wanted my kids to be well-behaved, polite and obedient, a reflection of my fabulous parenting, so I tried training them to listen to my every command. I thought I knew who my children should be and what they should do because I was older than them: I had more experience, so I knew best. Later, I realised my kids deserved to be treated with respect and needed to be loved unconditionally. I started accepting who they were and trusted that they would become the awesome people God created them to be.

I hoped my children would have strong faiths, and stay close to God, trusting Him rather than relying on themselves. I knew it was important that they use their God-given talents to make a difference in other people's lives. They also needed to find rewarding work that would support them.

Because it took me a long time to accept who I am and realise I'm okay, I wanted my kids to be comfortable with themselves, be confident and not worry about adapting to the crowd. I wanted them to have their own opinions, enjoy discussing them, and be open to new ideas.

I imagined my family working as a team, helping and encouraging each other and learning together.

I wanted my children to have big dreams and to work hard fulfilling them. To be open to possibilities, be excited by life, feel joy and be eager to share that with others. I hoped they'd be resilient and persevere through the inevitable difficult times.

Most of all, I wanted my kids to feel loved unconditionally and to love in return.

And all that has been possible because of unschooling. Our family knows this is the right way for us to live. So, even on difficult days, we have no choice: we must continue pulling together, encouraging, loving and forgiving one another.

But what about you? Do you wonder if unschooling works? Do you need some reassurance before you commit to this way of life? Or maybe you're unschooling but going through a difficult time, and your confidence has been dented. Or perhaps you've been distracted by the alternatives, and now you're wondering: *Is unschooling really the best way to raise and educate my kids? Does it work?*

Before we can decide whether unschooling works, we need to explore the word 'work'. What does it mean for you and your family? What do you hope will be the outcome of unschooling your kids?

The Challenge

1. Think about the following questions:

What are your hopes for your kids? Where would you like them to end up? Who do you want them to be?

Is academic success important to you? Do you have educational goals for your kids? Do you hope they will achieve good grades? Do you want them to have choices such as university? What about high-status careers? Is security rather than adventure important?

Perhaps you value obedience and the ability to follow instructions. Or would you like your kids to be self-motivated to work hard without you looking over their shoulders? Do you want your kids to question and think for themselves and have their own opinions rather than parroting yours, even if that could make you uncomfortable?

Do you want your children to love learning and be curious people? Is it important they use their talents? Should they live purposeful lives? Perhaps you want them to know they can make a difference. Do you want your kids to be excited by life and all its possibilities?

Do you have parental goals? How about your relationships with your kids? Are you willing to be friends with them? Or is friendship something that you want to reserve for the adult years? Do you hope you will always be close to your kids? Would you like them to be able to relate well to others? How about qualities such as compassion for others? Do you hope your kids will be generous, loving, kind and interested in other people?

Maybe you just want your kids to be happy? Do you want them to feel confident, know who they are and what they believe, and be able to stand up for themselves and what they think? Is this more important than fitting in with the crowd?

Is your faith a priority? Do you have values and beliefs you'd like to pass on to your kids? Do you want to surround them with beauty, truth and goodness? Do your kids need to learn to trust God and always be faithful?

2. Look at what you've written and evaluate your answers.

Do other people and their expectations influence any of your hopes and dreams? Do you want to impress and look like a 'good' parent? Are some of your hopes based on your needs rather than your children's?

3. Modify your answers until you are satisfied they reflect the true needs of your children and your family.

4. Ask these questions:

- Will unschooling my kids enable them to get where they want to go?

- Will it allow my family to do what is important?

- Will it work?

If you're unsure how unschooling works and what you can expect if you adopt this way of life, you could do some research. Read a few blogs. Talk to more experienced unschoolers. You could read my books *Curious Unschoolers* and *Radical Unschool Love*. Of course, you could complete the rest of the challenges in this book. Hopefully, they'll help you understand what unschooling is all about!

An Extra Challenge

There was one thing that wasn't on my original parental and educational wish list because it hadn't occurred to me that it was relevant: would unschooling change me into the person God created me to be?

Because of unschooling, I have continued learning and have had loads of unimagined fabulous adventures of my own. I've also changed. Although I'm not perfect, I'm no longer the dragon mother I used to be. We often see how we'd like others to grow and develop without realising that we need to grow too. Only when we start with ourselves is unschooling truly successful.

So, for this additional challenge, think about how you have changed because of your kids. You could also explore the areas where you still would like to grow.

How Will You Know if Unschooling Works?

Will you know it works if your children get into good universities, earn degrees, and then get high-status jobs that are well-paying, safe and secure? Will you grin with delight and say to those who criticised your way of life, "Look, unschooling works!" Will your friends and family be impressed? Will your children's achievements change their opinion about unschooling? Will you feel relieved that it all worked out?

Or will you know unschooling works when you're no longer tempted to control your kids by demanding they listen to your ideas, fulfil your expectations, do what you say and be the people you think they should be?

How about when you're not afraid to listen with interest to your kids, accepting their opinions instead of imposing yours on them?

Will you know unschooling works when you stop criticising and start accepting your unique and wonderfully made kids just as they are, loving them unconditionally?

Maybe you'll know when you no longer worry about what other people might say or think and are prepared to put your children first and stand up for them.

Will you know when you listen to the words falling from your lips and realise they are kind and full of respect?

Will you know unschooling works when you don't consider withdrawing your love to influence your children's behaviour?

When you're quick to forgive?

When you start trusting yourself as well as your kids?

How about when you like who you are and realise you're okay?

Will you know unschooling works when you regain your curiosity and want to learn more?

Perhaps you'll know when your heart flips over with love while looking at your children with wonder and awe.

Will you know when the doubts and fears disappear, and a feeling of profound peace washes over you, preventing you from doing anything else?

Will you know unschooling works when you look at yourself and recognise that you have changed and are no longer the person you used to be?

How will *you* know if unschooling works?

Related Reading

Does Unschooling Work? Curious Unschoolers

Accepting Ourselves and Our Kids: Radical Unschool Love

Treating Kids with Respect: Radical Unschool Love

How Unschooling Is about Both Parent and Child: Radical Unschool Love

4: Take Small Steps

You might know that my family unschooled in the early days of our homeschooling life, but it wasn't long before I started questioning what we were doing. If I had to stand back from my kids and let them learn entirely on their own, how would they ever hear about Shakespeare and other things I wanted to share with them? Would they stumble over all these rich experiences by themselves? Or would they miss out? I couldn't see how unschooling could work, so one day, we left it behind, and I began my search for the perfect way to educate my kids.

After circling through the various homeschooling methods again and again, I was finally ready to admit that none of them worked for our family. For just a moment, I was tempted to return to unschooling. My kids could learn by themselves, and I wouldn't have to do anything! I was tired, and this sounded attractive. But it also sounded irresponsible. So having rejected all the homeschooling methods and unschooling as well, I decided it was time for my family to 'do our own thing.'

One by one, I got rid of the things that weren't working for us until we got to a stage where we were all learning and thriving and happy. Life felt peaceful. Although I didn't at first realise it, we'd come full circle: we'd arrived at unschooling again. But this time, it was different. I discovered that unschooling isn't what I'd thought it was. I could get involved with my kids' learning. I could shout, "I'm going to watch *Hamlet*! Does anyone want to join me?" Yes, I was allowed to introduce my children to new things. Actually, doing that was essential. It's called strewing.

So, we got to unschooling by taking small steps, keeping the things we enjoyed and were important to us, and eliminating everything that wasn't answering our needs.

I find it reassuring that we can arrive at unschooling without ever intending to. This may indicate that unschooling is a very natural thing to do. What do you think?

You may like to approach unschooling in small steps too. Perhaps you're not ready to dive straight into unschooling but would rather take things slowly. But where do you start?

The Challenge

1. Look at your current situation and then list the positives.

What's working for your family? What do you enjoy? What brings you and your children joy?

This positive list will remind you to keep doing what works for your family. Your children might enjoy read-aloud books, going on outings, or reading poetry together. If so, that's wonderful. Do more of these things!

If you're new to unschooling, you might think you should drop everything you've been doing and make a fresh start, but that's not necessary. Keep doing the things you love.

2. List the negatives.

Are there things that are causing conflict in your family? What drains you of energy? What do you and your kids dread doing? What isn't fulfilling the current needs of your children?

3. Think carefully about your negative list. Are you doing some things for the wrong reasons?

Perhaps you do certain things out of fear.

Do you do certain things only because you want to impress your peers and be accepted by them? You may wish to gain the approval and acceptance of your family.

Do you do some things only because you want the education department to approve your kids' homeschool registrations?

Do you push your kids to do some things because you have trouble giving up your own ideas about who they should be and what they should do?

Do you have good reasons for doing things that don't feel right? Should you push on with them even if they cause conflict or unhappiness? Could you find better ways to do some things? Or could you stop doing them altogether?

4. Identify the one thing on your list that causes your family the most conflict or unhappiness. In other words, if you could change only one thing, what would it be?

Once you know where you'd like to start, can you make a change? Can you let go of something completely? Or do it differently?

Can you change something that isn't fulfilling the needs of your kids and take one small step deeper into unschooling?

An Extra Challenge

When it comes to our unschooling kids' learning, perhaps we're not always satisfied with small. We might not even notice the little things our children are achieving. Our eyes pass over the small while we're searching for the big. Small isn't good enough. We want to see impressive things to chase away our unschooling doubts. Maybe we also desire the big because we think it will impress others, squashing their criticism of how we've chosen to live.

So, for this extra challenge, why not focus on the small? Watch out for the little things. Take joy in them. Squash any feelings of disappointment that might be the result of hoping for big.

Here's an example of an occasion where I focused on the small, confident that the big achievement I was hoping for would follow in time if I didn't squash my daughter's enthusiasm:

Gemma-Rose is eager to show me a story she has written. She thrusts it into my hand and stands back, pleased with herself. I start to read and soon realise she has made many spelling mistakes. Do I say, "You'll have to work on your spelling," and then watch her face drop, risking she might never want to write again? Or do I ignore what she can't do and focus on her achievements? "That was a great story. I liked how you managed to rescue the mermaid from the cave. I didn't think she was going to escape!"

Sometimes I've needed reminding about the value of small achievements for myself. Years ago, I wanted to run 5 km, all at once, without stopping. When I couldn't do this overnight, I got discouraged and wanted to give up. But my wise husband, Andy, said, "Don't focus on what you *can't* do. Think about what you *can* do!" I soon realised that, although I couldn't run the distance I was aiming for, I was running further than I had run for a very long time. I'd achieve my goal eventually if I kept going. It didn't matter how long I took to get there, as long as I persisted.

In the same way, does it matter how long our kids take to arrive at their destination? They'll achieve the skills they need when they're ready. Unless, of course, we're not satisfied with the small and insist on the big and end up pounding our kids' enthusiasm for learning flat to the ground.

Related Reading

Why Unschooling Isn't a Method of Homeschooling: Curious Unschoolers

A Gradual Approach to Unschooling: Curious Unschoolers

Focusing on What We Can Do: Curious Unschoolers

5: Strew a Thing or Two

As I've said, at the beginning of our unschooling adventure, I yearned to share the things that interested me with my kids. But I thought that was against the unschooling 'rules'. (There was a lot about unschooling that I didn't understand.) I didn't realise it was essential to surround my kids with a rich environment by sharing things, ideas, thoughts and experiences with them. I had to look for resources associated with their passions or find something that might spark new interests. And, yes, I could invite my kids to share all the things that excited me. I was allowed to strew!

This book has a few strewing challenges because there are multiple ways to ignite our kids' curiosity and entice them to set off on exciting learning adventures. You could do this first strewing challenge whenever you want to add a spark to your family's learning. You could repeat it whenever your kids are looking around for something new to read, ponder, or investigate.

The Challenge

1. Walk around your house and look for potentially interesting items. You might find all kinds of things you've forgotten about hidden away in drawers, cupboards or on high shelves.

You might find something old like a music cassette. If you still have a cassette player, you could end up playing it and talking about music: how musicians used to sell their work before Spotify came along, favourite performers from years gone by, how technology changes, life when you were a teenager, and popular music shows and events. The possibilities are endless!

Do you have lots of unread books, unwatched DVDs and unplayed games?

You could hunt out some photo albums.

Do you have some craft supplies, clay, recipe books, balls of wool, beads, or packets of seeds? How about shells, postcards, a fountain pen or a picture of a famous painting?

2. Leave your chosen items in a prominent position.

On the kitchen table? On a coffee table? Somewhere else, where your family will see them?

3. You could let your kids stumble over your strewing by themselves.

4. Or you could offer an invitation or two. "Does anyone want to watch this movie with me?"

5. If no one is interested in the things you strew, you could use them yourself, which might lead to questions such as "What are you doing, Mum?" or "Can I watch that with you, Dad?"

6. After a week or two, repeat the challenge, replacing all the rejected items.

Related Reading

Time for Some Strewing: Curious Unschoolers

What to Do When Our Strewing Is Rejected: Curious Unschoolers

6: Reduce Unschooling Fears

We decide to unschool, and, for a time, everything goes well. Our kids are learning, our family bonds are strengthening, and life is full of joy.

Then one day, things change. Something happens. A child may make a mistake and choose to go her own way. She might do something we're not happy about. Doubts creep in, and we think that perhaps unschooling doesn't work. Maybe the critics are right: "You should have kept tight control over your kids!" Yes, we could feel like we've failed.

Or life is rolling along smoothly, but then we hear how well our friend's children are doing, and they're not unschoolers. We start playing the comparison game, and our kids end up losing. Again, we feel like we're failing.

Before we know it, our fears for our kids are ruling our days. We wonder if we're ruining our children's lives by unschooling. Is it time to do something more traditional? Will this increase our chances of success? And if it doesn't, and our kids fail regardless, who will blame us? We'd only have been doing what most people have done for a very long time.

Should we listen to our fears? Are they telling us something important? Or are they just distracting us from living a wonderful unschooling life with our kids?

The Challenge

1. Make a list of all your fears. Here are some common ones:

If we don't make our kids do things, they'll become lazy.

If we don't force them to do difficult things while growing up, they'll flounder when they set out into the bigger world where life doesn't revolve around them.

Unschooling won't prepare kids for their future lives. Unschoolers might not get into university. They could end up not being able to find secure jobs. It's better to make kids learn things they might not be interested in so all bases are covered.

If our kids are free to play video games for as long as they like, they'll become addicted.

Our kids won't learn how to behave if we instantly forgive them for their failings, so punishments are necessary.

2. Think about the things your kids might miss out on if you choose not to unschool.

Will your kids fail to learn to be responsible for their lives and education?

Will they rely on you to motivate them to learn or do what is right?

Perhaps they won't have opportunities to use their talents.

If they pursue safe and secure careers rather than following their passions, will they be happy?

They may learn because this is what is expected rather than because they love learning.

Will they learn to fear and not trust themselves?

Could they cling to what they have if they never experience abundance? Will they not be inclined to be generous with their time and possessions?

3. Find out more about unschooling. Our fears disappear when we gain a deeper understanding of its principles. You could read *Curious Unschoolers* and *Radical Unschool Love*!

4. Find a community of friendly, accepting and non-judgemental unschoolers who will answer your questions, address your concerns, share their experiences and encourage and support you.

5. Observe your kids. Talk with them and listen carefully. That's the best way to find out what they need!

6. You can do all the other challenges in this book!

7. If your fears still won't subside, think about these questions:

- What is the right way to live?

- What values are important to you?

- Do you believe kids deserve to be loved unconditionally?

- Should we accept them for who they are?

- Are our kids entitled to respect and kindness?

When you've decided on the values that you want to make the foundation of your family's life, think about this question:

Does unschooling match up with your values? Should you do it regardless of your fears? Is unschooling the right way for your family to live?

Related Reading

How to Deal with Criticism and Our Fears: Curious Unschoolers

When Unschooling Doesn't Seem to Be Working: Radical Unschool Love

Fearing Our Kids Will Fail: Curious Unschoolers

7: Ponder Educational Ideas

Most of us gained our ideas about how kids learn from our experiences at school. We were told that we needed teachers, we had to work our way through the course syllabus for each school subject in order, and our learning was graded. We were labelled as clever if we passed the various tests and examinations with high marks. We may have been given the impression that school was our one and only chance to get an education, so we had to learn certain things just in case we ever needed them. We were told that if we failed at school, we wouldn't be able to get into university and then get a secure job that was necessary if we wanted to be successful in life.

Unschooling turns all these educational ideas upside down by revealing the holes in most people's thinking. But it takes time to feel comfortable with new ideas. And it's hard to go against the crowd, isn't it? We could be hesitant to try unschooling even if it makes sense. Even when we decide that unschooling is the right thing for our family, the old ideas that we grew up with often remain at the backs of our minds, ready to push themselves forward whenever we're having a wobbly day and feeling insecure.

Can those old ideas be banished?

The Challenge

1. Make a list of the ideas causing you the most problems.

2. Think about how they relate to your childhood experiences.

You could start with a few questions from my book, *Curious Unschoolers*. The following questions come from the story called *Unlearning What We've Learnt About Education:*

Is it necessary to force kids to learn? Or are kids naturally curious people?

Is it even possible to force kids to learn? We may be able to persuade them to learn using bribes, rewards, shame or punishments, but is this real learning? Will children retain knowledge gained in this way? If they feel what they've learnt is irrelevant or uninteresting, will they let go of it as soon as they can: when the exam is over, when they've written the essay, when they've turned the page of the workbook? Is forcing kids to learn a waste of time?

As you ponder these questions, you could examine your childhood experiences. Were you forced to learn things that didn't seem relevant to you? How did your teachers persuade you to learn what you didn't want to know about? Were you ever rewarded for learning or punished for failing to learn? Did you ever let go of knowledge once an exam was over? Were there times when you were eager to learn? What made a difference? The topic? The teacher? Would you have liked more time to explore the things that interested you?

Are the ideas that governed your education true? Should you abandon some of them? Should you adopt a new way of thinking?

3. Jot down your thoughts. Hopefully, they'll encourage you to step into unschooling. Or they might refresh your resolve to keep unschooling the next time you feel insecure.

Sometimes we cling to particular ideas because they've been around for a long time. Or we think, "Why should I know better than most people?" But the truth of an idea can't be based on longevity or popularity. It has to withstand testing and critical thinking.

Of course, we often cling to old ideas even when we know they're false because it's hard doing something different from the crowd. It takes courage to stand alone. But our kids need us to be brave. If we're not, how will we help them with their needs? We'll always do what other people think is best rather than putting our kids first.

Related Reading

Unlearning What We've Learnt about Education: Curious Unschoolers

8: Become a Writer

My children noticed how much I enjoy playing around with words. They saw me jumping up and down with excitement when I successfully found the right words to express my thoughts. And they wanted to try too. They wanted to write.

Writing, like maths, can be a big worry, can't it? How will our kids learn to write if they don't do spelling and grammar exercises and practise writing stories and essays? Should children work on their writing skills in a structured way? Or will they learn to write when they have a need? Or an interest? Is our example important? Can we encourage a writing atmosphere in our homes similar to a reading one?

For this challenge, I'm inviting you to write, not your kids. Maybe you're thinking, "But I don't want to write! It's my kids who need to write, not me!" Perhaps this is a challenge that you're tempted to ignore. Or does the thought of writing make you feel excited?

It can be valuable to explore our feelings. If you're a reluctant writer, maybe this challenge will give you an insight into how your kids feel when you ask them to write. If you feel excited about writing, could your kids pick up on your feelings and want to write too? Enthusiasm is contagious!

So, will you write something? Will you do what you'd like your kids to do? Would you like to be a good example?

The Challenge

1. Choose your writing tools.

Will you use a computer, fountain pen, typewriter, marker, or pencil? What will you write on? A screen, fancy notebook, sheet of coloured paper, an unschool challenges notebook? Approached in the right way, this challenge could be a lot of fun!

2. Start writing.

It doesn't matter what you write. If you don't have any writing ideas, you could do some free writing by setting a timer and then writing about anything that comes to mind. The only rule is to keep writing. Don't stop. Just keep the words flowing onto your paper or screen, even if they seem silly or don't make much sense. Your piece of writing can be short, but once you start writing, you could find yourself wanting to continue even after the timer dings.

3. Share your writing.

Does the idea of sharing your words make you feel uncomfortable? Writing can seem like a very personal and private thing to do, can't it? Again, our hesitation to share might help us understand how our kids feel when we ask to see their writing but they don't want to show us. Should we respect each other's need to keep our writings to ourselves?

4. Write some notes about your writing!

Did you share your writing with your children or at least tell them about it? How did you feel before, during and after the challenge? Did you example inspire your kids? Will you continue writing now that you've completed this challenge?

Related Reading

My Writing Unrules: Curious Unschoolers

A Passion for Writing: Curious Unschoolers

9: Add Rhythm to Your Days

Years ago, when we first began unschooling, I thought that to unschool correctly, we had to get up (late) each morning and take the day as it came. Do whatever we felt like at each moment without thinking too far ahead. This sounded attractive - we were free to do whatever we liked! - but we soon found ourselves drifting through our days not achieving much, which was very unsatisfying. I needed to do something, so I added rhythm to our days. And that's what this unschooling challenge is all about.

Have you ever wondered about the connection between freedom and not wasting time? We have a limited number of hours, so we should make the most of them. But we don't want to live on a tight schedule, slotting activities into every minute of our days ahead of time.

We need to be free to make our own choices about what we do and when we do them. But what if we end up drifting through our days without purpose? What if we let ourselves get distracted away from what we want to do by such things as social media? We might think we're choosing how to spend our time, but is this true? Perhaps we're being controlled by whatever comes along. We're not living free lives after all because we're not directing our lives so that we achieve the things that mean the most to us.

Every so often, I think how wonderful it is that I'm free to get up each morning and do whatever I like. I might greet the day as it appears, not making plans, open to whatever comes along. And sometimes, this approach works out perfectly because we need to slow down, appreciate the things around us, and take advantage of the learning that presents itself to us at each moment. But if I live every day like this, I begin to feel dissatisfied because I never make progress on such things as my writing. I realise that I can't let life control me. I have to take charge of it. So I make a few loose plans, blocking out time for writing, exercising, and deliberately working on my skills.

We never mention planning when we're talking about unschooling, do we? Perhaps the two words don't seem to go together. Even now, I hesitate to link them. Maybe everyone will think I'm suggesting that we all structure our days and push our kids to do certain things (that we consider important). But that's not what I mean. The things that I'm suggesting we plan are those our kids want to do but, without some forethought, won't end up doing.

For example, our kids might want us to read books aloud, go on outings, and do crafts that need organising. Perhaps they want to do other things that need our help. Should we think ahead and block out time to get everything done?

My family used to use our mealtimes as markers in our days. There was a block of time before breakfast, another leading up to morning tea, one before lunch, and another that led to afternoon tea. We'd run along the bush tracks together during the before-breakfast time, do the chores, pray and read books aloud before morning tea. The rest of the day could vary, but usually, I had a free block of time between afternoon tea and dinner to blog and write.

At the beginning of each week, we'd make a few plans about such things as music lessons, outings, and appointments. I'd block them out mentally – somehow, I can keep things in my head – or write them on a calendar so they'd get done.

And every morning, after we'd completed the chores, I'd gather with my kids and talk about the day ahead. We'd discuss the routine things, such as what we would cook for dinner and any extra chores and errands we needed to do. I'd also say, "What will you do today? Is there anything special I can do for anyone? Does anyone need my help?"

Of course, we all have times when we need to go with the flow, such as periods of illness, the baby seasons of life, and when we're dealing with crises. But ordinarily, it's good to think carefully about how we spend our time so that we're free to do what's important to us. We should direct our lives instead of letting them direct us.

How do we encourage our kids to direct their lives so that they accomplish their goals? Or maybe we don't have to worry because they could already be good at doing this. Kids are curious people who want to learn. They can concentrate while diving deep into whatever interests them, immersing themselves in games, books, research, and other activities. They have things they want to do, and they get on and do them. Unless we distract them.

School bells and structured lesson plans cut a child's life into pieces which must be very frustrating when they're working deeply. And it can be so easy to undervalue our kids' activities and attempt to divert them away from them. Similarly, we might not recognise that rest and thinking times are essential. We might want to say, "Stop wasting your time and go do something more productive!" We could want to direct our kids instead of allowing them to work out for themselves what's the best way to spend their time.

We may have trouble believing our kids can direct their lives because we, the parents, often get distracted by whatever is happening around us. We let life take us where it will. To pass on the true meaning of freedom to our kids, do we need to think carefully about the purpose of our days and take control? Is our example important?

Saying all this, we should always retain the freedom to let go of our loose plans because sometimes unexpected things happen that are far more important than the work we intend to do. I'd rather remain at the kitchen table long after lunch is over, listening to a daughter, instead of writing a planned blog post. Even though we're big Shakespeare fans, we'd all prefer to postpone watching a play together if the sun suddenly reappears and shouts, "It's a picnic kind of day!"

So what do you think? Should we think about how we're spending our time? Is it okay to make plans? Are they just a normal part of life?

And does adding rhythm to our days allow us to direct our lives instead of letting them direct us?

The Challenge

1. Get together with your family and decide what's important to you and your kids.

Do you want to exercise each morning, pray, do the chores, read books aloud, spend time with each child, practise the piano, have outside music lessons, work on your own projects, walk the dog, meet up with friends, or write in your journals?

2. Divide your days into blocks without necessarily involving hours and minutes.

This isn't a scheduling challenge where we write down what we want to do at every moment of the day.

3. Add your activities to your days.

Once you have a loose idea of what your days need to look like, think about the activities you've decided you'd like to do.

If your kids want you to read to them, do you have your books close to hand? Do you have things to strew? If your kids would like to go on more outings, do you have some ideas of places to visit? Do you know what you'll do when you get some free time for yourself? Do you need a personal strewing basket? (You could do the strewing basket challenge!)

The Rhythm 'Rules'

1. Rhythm isn't about rules, structure and scheduling every minute of the day. It's about slotting in some regular activities you and your children want to do.

2. A rhythm has to fulfil the needs of everyone in the family. And it has to be flexible because needs can change over time. They might even change from hour to hour. Also, when we're unschooling, we want to take advantage of unexpected opportunities: continue interesting conversations, go on spur-of-the-moment adventures, accept invitations, rest because we're tired, or follow a rabbit trail we suddenly find ourselves drawn along.

3. A rhythm isn't about parents getting kids to do everything parents consider essential. It's about everyone having the opportunity to do what's important to them. So if parents want to run before breakfast, that's what we should do. If our kids would like to join us, they can. If they'd rather sleep, then that's okay too. Slotting our shared activities into our days means finding times that suit everyone.

4. A rhythm isn't something established by a parent that a family lives by. It's developed naturally or intentionally by everyone in the family. It's the way we want to live our lives together.

5. A rhythm can't compromise our family's freedom to choose: it can't limit what we do. It can't take the adventure out of unschooling!

If you want to live an amazingly free life with your family while achieving all the things that are important to you and your kids, why not add some rhythm to your days?

Living an Ordered Christian Life

God has given us a finite amount of time, so shouldn't we make the most of our days by living an ordered life? Perhaps we should make every minute count by planning our lives carefully. Or is an ordered life not scheduled minute-by-minute but built on a foundation of prayer instead?

We must be faithful daily with our prayers, taking time to talk with God and read the Bible and other spiritual books. Life can sometimes get overwhelmingly busy. We might neglect our prayer life and start to live in a disordered way, doing what we think is best without any thought of God. Maybe we don't even consider that we might need His help. But if we pray consistently, putting God first in our lives, the Holy Spirit can guide us: we listen, learn to trust God and receive His unconditional love, which enables us to love our family and friends the same way.

But prayer alone isn't enough. We need to live our faith and make it visible in our lives: our kids need to see us praying, reading our Bibles and making decisions and reacting to everything that happens to us through the lens of our faith. We have to approach prayer with joy rather than with duty. Our faith has to become like the air we breathe. It's essential, and we can't help sharing it with our family. It has to be the foundation of our lives.

Everything will flow from that foundation. We won't need to schedule our lives tightly out of fear. Instead of controlling our own lives and those of our kids, we'll want to trust God and go where He leads. Sometimes this might not look ordered on the surface, but underneath, could God have everything in hand? Could His ideas be bigger than those contained in our plans? Will we know we're living ordered lives when we feel at peace?

10: Learn Not to Fear Failure

I once heard a priest say something along the lines of:

Fear indicates that an opportunity has arrived.

He also said:

We are made for adventure.

The big question is this:

When we're afraid, will we be courageous, grab the opportunity that has arrived, and set out on an adventure? Or will our fears paralyse us? Will the fear of failure cause us to miss out on something that could be amazing?

I have had lots of failures. Here's one of them:

Years ago, when our eldest child was 12, we moved to a cottage on a 100-acre property so my kids could live a free, wild, rich, unschooling life. We wanted to grow our own food and have a goat, some chooks, and even a donkey. But nothing went to plan. The soil was too poor for growing vegetables. It hardly ever rained, so we had to pay for water to be trucked to our home. We had to deal with rats and mice. My husband couldn't get a job within reasonable travelling distance of the property. Our one and only neighbour threatened to shoot our dog if it jumped over our connecting fence. And then our unborn baby was diagnosed with 'an abnormality incompatible with life'. We ended up back in town, grieving the loss of our son.

So many worries and difficulties. Our move to the country seemed like a total failure. But it wasn't. As we endured all the hardships we hadn't anticipated, we learnt about the important things of life while growing closer together as a family. We realised that we can't give our kids a perfect life, however hard we try, but we can give them love. That's what they need more than anything else. We also learnt that our ideas aren't always the right ones. We have to let go of control and trust. Trust God and each other.

We also learnt not to fear failure.

The Challenge

1. Write down your fears.

Are they legitimate? What if you do fail? Would it be as big a deal as you imagine?

2. List some of your failure stories. We all have them!

Did anything good come out of your failures? Was the failure a stepping stone to something else? Even if it was difficult, can you see how you've grown because of the experience?

3. Think about your current situation.

Is fear standing in the way of you setting out on what could be an incredible adventure? Should you move forward despite your fear? Because what is the worst that could happen? Things might not go according to your plan. You could end up somewhere different to where you'd hoped to be, but would that be so bad? Your unexpected destination might be better than the one you'd been hoping for. And if it isn't, you will have learnt a lot, at the very least. We need to move if we want to grow, don't we?

4. Do your experiences of failure prevent you from encouraging your kids to try out their ideas and reach for their dreams? Do you want to keep them safe rather than let them expose themselves to possible criticism? Perhaps you don't want them to feel the negative emotions that could result from failure, feelings that you probably have had to deal with?

It's hard for us to step back and allow room for failure, isn't it? But it's something we must do. It's the way our kids learn and grow.

The Ultimate Failure

Perhaps most people regarded Jesus' death on the cross as a failure. The disciples had such great hopes. They never imagined Jesus being crucified, and after His death, they thought everything was finished. That was the end of the story. Jesus' mission seemed to be the ultimate failure. But, of course, it wasn't! What looked like failure was salvation for the world.

So, I'm wondering if we should be courageous, do what we feel is right, and not worry about failure. Trust. Even if things don't turn out as we imagine, it doesn't mean we have failed. Perhaps we are where God intends us to be. Even if we make decisions that weren't in God's plan for us, if we turn to Him, He will turn our failures into something good.

Of course, it would be better if we did God's will straightaway rather than follow our own ideas. But how do we know what He wants us to do? Could we have to listen more carefully to His voice? Make a habit of listening so that His voice becomes familiar? Then when we have big decisions to make, we'll hear what we should do.

We're good at listening to our own voices, aren't we? But do we need to put aside our ideas and thoughts so we can hear God more clearly? And should we become more familiar with our children's voices too? Often we talk over the top of them. If their voices don't fit in with our plans, we ignore them. Sometimes all we can hear are our words. We need to be quiet so we can hear our kids. And so we can listen to God.

Related Reading

Is Our Unschooling Life Rich Enough?: Radical Unschool Love

Fearing Our Kids Will Fail: Curious Unschoolers

11: Turn Unschooling into Homeschool Records

When my kids were homeschooling unschoolers, we sometimes had quiet days at home. There was plenty of time to say such things as, "Would you like to watch a Shakespeare play with me?" We read books and drank hot chocolate. We wrote and chatted and worked on our individual projects. And as we did all this, I added links, photos, and notes to our homeschool records book.

At other times, life raced along at an incredible pace. We took trips away from home, my girls attended music lessons, we shopped and ran errands, we took recycling to the resource centre, and we chose paint to decorate our house's interior. We attended music recitals, took a new puppy to the vet, went on outings to scout for new music video locations, and filmed videos. One thing after another.

In the evenings, we'd flop onto the sofa to watch a movie or a TV show together (nothing 'educational'), and I'd wonder: "How am I going to turn our busy unschooling day into homeschool records notes?" Could I translate all my kids' real-life activities into the educational language required by our state? Yes, I could.

During the 28 years or more of registered homeschooling, I never had a problem satisfying the representative from the education department who visited our home every couple of years. I presented my children's unschool learning in a way that impressed and convinced her beyond a doubt that they were receiving an outstanding education.

You may also be legally required to keep homeschool records. Like us, you might have to turn your busy unschooling life into something the authorities will recognise as education. If so, this may be a challenge for you.

And even if you don't have to keep homeschool records, you could still do this challenge. It might help you see how much learning your kids are experiencing while living their lives.

The Challenge

1. Find out what your education department requires.

Are your kids expected to follow your state's school syllabus? Print out or make a digital copy of these requirements. It's good to look like we know what we're doing!

In our state of NSW, we had to provide evidence that our kids were learning about the topics in the school syllabus related to the Key Learning Areas of maths, English, science, history and geography, creative arts, personal development, health and physical education (PDHPE).

2. Find a method of homeschool record keeping that will showcase all your kids' unschool learning.

The best approach is the one that will allow you to record the many different ways your kids learn. A visually attractive system is a bonus. And the method needs to be quick and easy to use. You don't want to spend too much of your day keeping records!

I chose to use Evernote, but other digital notebook apps will work. Or you could stick to a paper journal.

3. Think about how you can record your kids' learning without using the usual workbooks, and spelling and other tests.

Here are some ideas for things you can add to your notebook:

- Cover images of read-aloud and other books

- Blurbs of books read

- Screenshots of books borrowed from the public library

- Promotional images of movies and documentaries watched

- Description of each movie or documentary

- Personal star rating for each book and movie

- Photos or scans of recipes

- Movie, concert, and outing tickets or photos of them

- Photos of concert programs

- Google maps of places visited and places mentioned in novels, movies and documentaries

- Videos of your kids singing, cooking, playing, experimenting, exercising

- Links to YouTube videos you've watched

- Copies of articles you've read

- Notes about conversations you've had with your kids

- Photographs of everything: outings, games, practising the piano, the oven temperature and the percentage of Kindle books read (maths), shopping, crafts

- Images of famous artworks you've enjoyed

- Descriptions of artworks: copy and paste online info

- Audio files of bird calls, kids playing instruments and singing, the music you've listened to

- Occasional audio clips or videos of your musicians giving short concerts

- Screenshots of games and other online activities

- Copies of poems you've enjoyed

4. Add notes to your notebook.

Add lots of them. Your overflowing notebook will impress your education department representative. It will also be stuffed full of things you will want to remember. Your homeschool records notebook could double up as your family journal.

5. Give a title to each of your kids' learning notes.

Creative titles might be fun, but I chose to use the relevant school subjects. When our Authorised Person (AP) examined our notes, she saw at a glance that my kids were learning lots of science, maths, and English.

6. If you're keeping digital records, add tags to each note.

I added the school subjects and extra tags such as 'photography', 'outings', 'novels', and 'videos'. I could search for a particular tag, and only the related notes would appear onscreen. Again, this is useful if an AP wants to see only the science notes or the English ones. Of course, if you've also tagged your notes with your children's names, you'll be able to search for each child's science, English or maths notes.

Some Extra Tips

Even if you're happy to keep homeschool records, you don't want to spend all day recording your kids' learning experiences. So how do you prevent record-keeping from taking over your life and becoming a chore? Here are a few ideas for using a digital system such as Evernote.

1. Use one notebook for all your children instead of trying to keep separate records for each child. Tag your notes with the appropriate child's name.

2. Use as few notebooks as possible. I started with weekly notebooks but then decided to have only one notebook for each term of the school year. Because I didn't have to make each week look equally productive, I was more relaxed and didn't worry about quiet weeks. Things evened out over the course of each term. Stack your notebooks, putting each year's notebooks into one bundle, so everything is easy to find.

3. Record as much as possible 'on the go'. It's very time-consuming and tiring doing record keeping at the end of the day. Also, you might forget some of the details!

4. Take and import photos from mobile devices. Don't worry about editing them.

5. Keep your device handy and add a note here and there throughout the day. Add notes while drinking your morning coffee!

6. Add Evernote to all your devices so that your PCs, tablets and phones sync.

7. Copy and paste similar notes instead of writing new ones. Because it took us several weeks to finish each read-aloud book, I used the same reading note multiple times.

8. Links to websites, Youtube videos, and articles can be clipped while on the sites immediately after viewing or reading.

9. Quickly jot down notes about activities and conversations as they happen, if possible. If you want to make your notes more attractive, you can add images, icons and other information later. And if there's no time for locating appropriate images, it doesn't really matter. The words are the most important bit.

10. Although I suggested you make lots of notes, you don't have to record every learning experience. As long as you have enough notes to satisfy the education department and you've captured the memories that are important to your family, you've done enough.

11. Record keeping will get quicker once you've established your system and know what you want to record and how you will do it.

There might be times when record-keeping seems like a burden. You may wish you weren't required to do it. But it's not all bad, especially if you use an effective method to capture all those wonderful learning experiences you'd like to remember forever.

Also, record-keeping will encourage you to be observant. You will need to keep your eyes open for learning experiences to prevent your notebooks from looking bare. And that means you'll notice every little stage of your children's growth and development, every small achievement. Time won't pass in a blur. You will live in the moment.

The most important aspect of record keeping is adopting a positive attitude because complaining about a situation we can't change is very draining. Strange as it may seem, I enjoyed record-keeping once I began viewing our Evernote notebooks as our family's journal. I started looking for new ways to make it attractive, knowing that, one day, we'd scroll back through my notes, saying such things as:

"Do you remember when you read *Ballet Shoes* to us, Mum?"

"Wasn't that a fantastic day when we went to the beach?"

"Can we watch that video of us singing together again? That was years ago! Haven't we changed a lot?"

Those memories are precious!

Related Reading

Using a Gentle Approach to Change People's Minds about Unschooling: Curious Unschoolers

12: Listen to Kids

Being a good listener is easy, isn't it? All we have to do is stay quiet while other people talk. Well, that's what I used to believe. It wasn't until I took a counselling course that I realised I was a terrible listener.

I'd let my mind wander while my husband told me about his day. Or I'd be so busy composing what I wanted to say when I got the chance that I didn't listen to his part of a conversation.

Or I'd want to jump in and tell my kids they were wrong before they'd finished what they were saying. I'd interrupt when they shared their difficulties: "You'll be okay! Things aren't that bad!' I wanted to reassure them before I'd heard the whole story, not realising I was sweeping away my kids' feelings.

Or I'd decide what someone was saying to me without listening to their actual words. I'd filter conversations through my experience and assume I knew what they were saying. Or I'd change the topic of a conversation because I believed what I wanted to say was far more interesting.

When we listen properly, we take a genuine interest in the other person. We show them they are important. We want to know what they think, what they're interested in, and who they are. Taking an interest in other people makes us more interesting. Isn't that interesting?

We all know when someone is listening to us properly, don't we? Good listeners listen with their bodies, turning to face us, leaning forward with eye contact. They reflect what we're saying so we can confirm that they've heard correctly. If they've got the wrong end of the stick, we have an opportunity to rephrase things.

So we know how to listen, but who should we listen to?

Often we run this way and that, reading books and blogs and listening to other people, trying to work out how best to parent our children. But we sometimes forget to listen to the most important people in our lives: our kids. If we do listen, we'll discover their needs and dreams, what's important to them, and what they're thinking. We'll find out that kids are deep thinkers who have amazing ideas. They can teach us so much, giving us a fresh perspective on life:

One of the huge delights of my unschooling life is sitting quietly with my children while chatting together.

I'm good friends with my kids. We're always sharing our thoughts, ideas, stories, dreams, problems, and moments of joy. We don't talk so I can impress my opinions on my children. I don't tell them what I think and, therefore, what they should think. Instead, I'm interested in what they have to say. Who are they? What ideas do they have? What thoughts are circling through their minds?

I love listening to my kids. They observe. They think deeply. I am continually surprised by their wisdom.

My unschooling children give me a fresh perspective on life. They help me see things more clearly. Is this because they aren't tied down by those old ideas that sometimes echo in my head?

Our kids can learn from us, but we can also learn from them. If we are prepared to listen.

The Challenge

Listen to your kids. Listen with your whole body and attention. Perhaps you can arrange some one-on-one time with each of your children.

Of course, we can't force children to share. We don't want to make them feel like we're waiting for them to tell us everything possible. But we can open up some opportunities for our kids to talk, show them we're interested, and if they respond, we can listen.

Related Reading

A Fresh Perspective: Radical Unschool Love

13: Be Adventurous

Maybe there are times when we wish our kids would be more adventurous:

"How do you know you don't like it? You haven't tasted it! "

"I'm sure you'll enjoy yourself once you get there."

"You'll have fun if you join in."

Yes, we urge our kids to be brave and try new things. But what about us? Are we adventurous parents? Or do we stick to what we know and sit on the sidelines of life where it's safe? We may miss out on all kinds of enjoyable experiences because we're too embarrassed or scared or set in our ways to get involved or try new things.

Years ago, while at a homeschooling camp, my kids wanted me to run in the mothers' race at the sports carnival. At first, I refused to join in. I wanted to stay with the mothers who had their arms crossed in front of their bodies as they firmly shook their heads. I gave my kids excuses: "I'm too old! And look at my clothes. I'm not dressed for running."

Then seeing the disappointed looks on my children's faces, a wild thought came into my head. Should I be daring, throw caution to the wind and do the unexpected? I imagined flying through the air, my children cheering me on. I knew I'd feel wonderful as I crossed the finish line.

Unfortunately, things didn't turn out as I hoped. A few metres into the race, my feet slipped from underneath me. I did the unexpected: I flew towards the ground and landed in the dirt.

For a few moments, I wished I hadn't been adventurous. I was dirty, I'd grazed my knees and my hands, and I was embarrassed. Did everyone see me go splat on the ground?

My kids saw me fall, but they didn't turn red like me. They didn't look around to see who'd witnessed their mother landing in an undignified heap in the dirt. After making sure I was still in one

49

piece, Imogen said, "We're so proud of you, Mum. You were willing to give it a go."

Those words made me feel so warm inside. After hearing them, I said, "Next year, I'm not going to run in boots. I am going to wear proper running shoes." Yes, I wanted to try again.

Being adventurous is worth the risk because we might discover it's fun to step out of our comfort zones rather than sit safely on the sidelines of life. And if we do fall splat in a heap and turn red, embarrassment won't kill us.

The Challenge

1. Make a list of adventurous things you could do.

You can start small. You don't have to parachute out of a plane or bungee jump. Or run in a mother's race!

You could:

- Take a walk in the rain, jump in a few puddles, and refuse to worry about wet hair. It will dry!

- Choose a cafe you've never visited, and don't order your usual coffee or tea. Instead, try something different.

- Buy and cook a type of food you've never tasted.

- Accept an invitation to play a game that's not really your thing.

- Read a book or watch a movie that isn't your usual genre. Ask your kids for some suggestions!

- Take a selfie and not worry about wrinkles, messy hair or whether you feel fat or thin.

- Be extra adventurous and make a selfie video.

- Wear something striking. Put on some makeup, paint your nails bright, or wear big earrings.

- Drive or walk somewhere via a different route than usual. See the world from a different angle.

- Try a new activity. Learn a new skill.

- If possible, go somewhere by yourself. Instead of waiting until someone wants to go to the park, explore a trail, visit a new cafe, attend an exhibition or see a movie at the cinema, go by yourself and have a solo adventure. Swing on the swings, hike through the bush, drink coffee, take photos, munch popcorn and enjoy your own company.

- Eat dessert before dinner.

- Say yes instead of no.

- Skip instead of walking.

- Run for a few metres and feel the wind in your hair.

- Sing.

- Laugh loudly.

- Be bold.

- Be silly.

- Have fun.

- Step out of your comfort zone just a little.

- Don't worry about what others might think.

2. When you have written your list, choose something on it.

Be adventurous!

My kids grin whenever I'm adventurous. They love seeing me having fun and often want to join in. Our example encourages our kids to give things a go!

Related Reading

The Splat: Radical Unschool Love

Being Brave, Adventurous and Just a Bit Daring: Radical Unschool Love

14: Strew Directly

How do you strew the resources that might interest your kids? Do you place them on a table and hope your children will stumble over them in their own time? What if there's something you really hope they will notice?

When my kids were younger, I often found a book, movie or other item I was eager to share with them. I was excited by the resource and wondered if it would excite them too. And then there were occasions when I didn't have time to wait until my children discovered a resource in their own time. The moment had arrived to use it. I needed to know immediately if they wanted to get involved.

So, sometimes, I strewed directly. I'd ask some questions, such as:

"Would you like to watch this movie with me?"

"I enjoyed this book. Would you like to read it too?"

"I feel like watching a Shakespeare play. Want to join me?"

"I'm going for a walk around the lake. Would you like to come along?"

"Would you like to hear what I found out?"

"I found a game that sounds good. Shall I tell you about it?"

"I found some new cake recipes. Do you feel like doing some baking?"

"That looks interesting. Would you like me to help you find out more?"

"I heard there are some whales at the beach. Shall we go and see them?"

Is it okay to strew directly? Or is it against the unschooling 'rules'? I think it's quite alright to draw our kids' attention towards particular resources and experiences as long as they are free to accept or reject our suggestions!

The Challenge

1. Make a list of possible strewing questions.

Have these questions on the tip of your tongue, ready to use at appropriate moments.

2. Find something that you're eager to share with your children.

3. Offer it to them using a question.

I hope your strewing is successful, but if it isn't, try again. There are limitless things we could strew directly!

Related Reading

Time for Some Strewing: Curious Unschoolers

15: Explore Screen Time

Should we give our kids unlimited access to their devices? Or is that irresponsible? Perhaps you're not sure. Maybe you sway from one point of view to another, depending on your kids' behaviour, what you read, or who you're talking to? Would it be good to explore this issue and clarify your thoughts and feelings?

The Challenge

1. Find a pen and paper or open your device.

2. Set a timer for ten minutes.

3. Free write about screens, pouring your thoughts onto the page or screen without stopping.

What aspect of screen time will you write about? Your fears about unlimited screen time? Your worries about possible addiction? Are you concerned about your kids living balanced lives? Are there things you feel they are missing out on while they're busy on their devices?

You may head in the opposite direction and explore the positives of technology. What do screens allow kids to do? Have amazing opportunities opened up because of the Internet and devices?

Will you write about yourself? How do you use screens? Do they connect you? Or perhaps they distract you?

It doesn't matter where you start. You just need to write and not stop until your time is up.

4. Read what you've written. You may discover an idea or thought that's worth exploring in more depth.

5. Take an idea or thought that you'd like to continue exploring and free write about it.

Here's what appeared when I sat down to write about screen time:

What if our kids want unlimited reading time instead of unlimited screen time? Imagine them spending every available hour with their heads in a book. They might ignore the chores. They might read secretly in bed under the blankets when they should be asleep. Getting them out of bed the next day might be challenging. What if they don't want to go outside and exercise? Or join in with family activities? They might only be interested in their books.

We might say:

"You never do anything but read."

"You'll ruin your eyesight looking at a page all day."

"Go outside and exercise!"

"You never talk to me. You're always reading!"

"Put that book down and pay attention!"

"What are you reading? That book looks like a waste of time!"

We might worry that:

Reading is a solitary activity (though we might share our books and thoughts with someone later).

It doesn't involve physical activity (unless we try to balance a book on the treadmill).

Books are addictive because sometimes we have to keep turning the pages. They could be impossible to put down.

But despite all these negative aspects of reading, no one seems to worry if kids want to read all day. We're proud of our readers:

"He's always got a book in his hand!"

"You won't believe how many books my daughter has read!"

Why is unlimited reading acceptable? Could we have discovered the value of reading?

Or could we have moved our concerns onto something new? We've got unlimited screen time to worry about these days, haven't we?

What else will come along to challenge our thinking? One day, will we say, "I wish he'd play on his device instead of..."?

6. To finish this challenge, jot down some thoughts about the following questions:

- What did you discover?

- Were you surprised by the words that poured onto your page?

- Did you end up somewhere unexpected?

- Did you learn something about your kids?

- Or perhaps about yourself?

Our ideas can change over time, can't they, even though we're sure they won't? Our kids grow, we have new experiences, we ponder unschooling more deeply, and we understand better. So this may be a challenge you can return to more than once. Wouldn't it be interesting if your thoughts lead you to a different place the second time around?

Related Reading

Is it Really Okay to Give Kids Unlimited Access to Screens and the Internet?: Curious Unschoolers

Watching TV, Playing Computer Games, Doing Nothing Much at All: Curious Unschoolers

Are Computer Games a Waste of Time?: Curious Unschoolers

16: Create a Strewing and Planning Notebook

For over 28 years, homeschooling registration was at the forefront of my mind. To fulfil homeschooling requirements, I had to prove my kids were learning the topics in the school syllabus. I also had to submit a homeschooling plan to the education department. How could we do that if we were unschooling and didn't know from day to day what we'd be doing?

In the early years of homeschooling, as part of our registration preparation, I wrote a plan for one term, choosing some topics from the syllabus that I thought would interest my kids and told our Authorised Person (AP), "I will plan subsequent school terms in the same way." Often, we didn't use our submitted plan because my kids wanted to do something completely different. But this was okay. No one ever checked that we used my plans, and if someone had, I'd have said, "My kids' needs changed, so I changed the plan."

It can seem like a waste of time writing plans we'll probably never use, can't it? That's why I continued to think about the problem. Could I find a better solution? When I started using Evernote, I had an idea. I created a digital notebook with two functions: strewing and planning.

I filled the notebook with ideas and resources I hoped might attract my children's attention: videos, books, websites, links of all kinds, and even photos of things we own. My girls had access to that notebook. They browsed it whenever they were looking for something to learn. I browsed it, too, because there were times when I was also looking for a good book to read, a video to watch or a skill I could gain. My strewing notebook was bursting with notes that led us on some fabulous learning adventures.

This notebook also doubled up as a planning notebook when registration time rolled around. When the AP asked, "Have you made a plan for the next two years? How will you cover the school syllabus? What resources will you use?" I opened my digital notebook and said, "We plan to use these resources. They cover the syllabus."

At regular intervals, I looked at the school syllabus to see what the education department expected my kids to learn. I knew my girls would naturally cover some of these topics while pursuing their interests. But there were always gaps that I had to fill. So I searched for engaging resources to cover these areas. I found books, movies, games or something similar. (Usually not textbooks!) I then clipped links to all these into the planning notebook and labelled each note with the appropriate school subject. And then the notes waited for my children to discover them. Often I pointed the way to some of them.

So I offered my children many opportunities to learn what was in the school syllabus by putting together a notebook of resources. They were free to use what I'd found or ignore my suggestions. Usually, my girls were very interested. Their eyes would light up even when I presented them with required topics. Just because something is in the syllabus doesn't automatically make it boring. The syllabus is actually stuffed full of things that are very interesting indeed. It just depends on how you learn about them, what resources you use, and if you are free to approach them how and when you like.

But there were inevitably some things that didn't interest my kids. They didn't want to learn about everything in the school plan. What did I do? Did I say, "You have to learn about this... and that... and the other because it's required"? No. We can offer children learning opportunities but can't make them learn. Learning is an active activity and requires cooperation on the part of the learner. We can't force knowledge into a child's head, though many people spend a lot of time trying. I decided that as long as I'd offered my kids opportunities to learn everything in the syllabus, I'd fulfilled the homeschooling registration requirements. There was no more I could do.

After one of our registration visits, our AP stopped as she was leaving, waved her arm towards the houses further down the street and said, "No one knows about the amazing things happening behind your door!" She'd been very impressed by what she'd seen in our Evernote notebooks.

We said goodbye to our AP and returned inside with huge grins on our faces. We'd done it again. We'd got through another registration visit, fulfilling all the requirements without compromising our unschooling way of life. Of course, I'd had to do some clever 'planning' in my notebook. But I'd been happy to do this. All the effort involved was worth it. Not only did it help us get through the registration visit, but it also produced a notebook packed full of resources that my girls and I continually dipped into.

The Challenge

This challenge is designed for a digital notebook, but with some extra work and thought, you might be able to adapt it for a paper record-keeping system.

1. Find out what your state's homeschooling requirements are.

Do your kids need to learn what's in the school syllabus? Or are they free to learn whatever they like?

2. Make a copy of the homeschooling requirements and the school syllabus.

Place them in a notebook labelled *Syllabus*. You'll need this notebook when you're looking for resources. Also, the notebook will show your education department representative that you are aware of the requirements you are supposed to fulfil.

3. Create a notebook for your resources.

I called our notebook our planning notebook because I wanted our AP to regard it as our homeschool plan. However, I always considered it our unplanning or strewing notebook.

4. Add resources associated with your kids' interests to the notebook: websites, books, articles, YouTube videos, movies, documentaries, online classes and programs, apps, magazines, music, and images.

5. Add resources for things that excite you and might also appeal to your kids.

6. Add resources that are associated with topics in the school syllabus.

I never tried to cover the whole syllabus. I added a resource here and one there, and my notebook grew over time. It was always a work in progress.

7. Label each resource note with the appropriate school subject.

8. When your AP visits and asks if you have written a homeschooling plan for the next registration period, open your notebook, put it in front of her, and say, "This is our planning notebook. It contains resources that cover the school syllabus. My kids will be using some of them."

I never promised we'd use all the resources in our notebook, but I was sure many of them would indeed interest my kids.

Of course, your notebook, like mine, won't cover everything in the school syllabus, but that's okay. Your AP probably won't check to see if there are resources for every topic, but if she is concerned, you could tell her the notebook is a work in progress, so you're continually adding to it.

9. Whenever one of your children uses a resource from your planning and strewing notebook, copy its note into your current term's homeschooling record-keeping notebook.

Putting together a strewing and planning notebook could seem like a lot of work, especially when you first start. You might wonder how you will create enough notes to impress an AP. But you'll be amazed how quickly they will multiply. Just think about Pinterest boards. They soon fill up, don't they? We find a link we want to save and then another one. Before we know it, our board is overflowing with things that excite us. Our notebooks will be the same. I guess we could use Pinterest boards instead of a notebook. That's definitely an option you could consider. I decided Evernote is more versatile, but Pinterest might work for you!

Related Reading

How We Unschool Despite Having to Fulfil Homeschool Registraion Requirements: Curious Unschoolers

17: Learn by Experiencing

Years ago, when my kids shared their knowledge with me, I'd say, "Where did you learn that?" How did they gain those facts, thoughts, ideas, or skills without me? Wasn't I an essential part of the learning process? It turned out that my input was less important than I'd thought. Oh yes, my kids relied on me to take them on outings, and they needed my help to get to the library, and sometimes they required resources that only I could provide. But even without my involvement, they could learn plenty on their own. They learnt while they were experiencing the everyday world around them.

We might think we have to teach our children about such things as forces, gravity, density, heat conduction, friction, the seasons, energy, and life cycles. But even if we never mention these things, our kids will still learn much about them. Kids might not be able to name Newton's Laws of Motion, but they will learn how forces work while pushing each other on the swings, tugging heavy boxes, and feeling the strength of the waves while playing in the ocean. They know about gravity because they leap and swing and bounce. Jumping in puddles teaches them about the transfer of energy, and so does running on hot sand. Kids experience friction by attempting to walk on ice or a wet floor or hauling a heavy cart along a rocky path. They know it's better to throw a ball than a feather to a friend. They can smell the salt in the sea air. Each year, they live through the seasons with all their changes. They know that rain falls from clouds and the sun can burn skin.

We could spend a day at the beach or a playground or hiking through a forest and come home thinking that our kids have done nothing but get some exercise while enjoying themselves. We might assume we have no notes for our homeschool records books. What could we possibly write? All our kids did was have some fun. But it's amazing: while they're playing and enjoying themselves, children are soaking up all kinds of learning. They're observing and listening, touching and smelling. They might even be tasting. (All my kids ate a few snails when they were toddlers!) They're also experimenting as they work out how the world operates.

Even though our kids can learn without us, we might still want to share what we know. But how do we do that without taking over?

Instead of thinking of ourselves as knowledge transmitters, we could focus on being fellow explorers of the world. Just like our kids, we need to be curious people, approaching the world with awe and wonder. Fellow explorers share their discoveries. They get excited, and that excitement is contagious. They ponder questions. Why do we see worms after it has rained? Why do some trees drop their leaves in autumn? They want to know more!

We need to slow down and take delight in our kids' discoveries. If they ask questions, we should take the time to answer them or research the answers together. We should listen to our kids and say, "Tell me more!" They may be open to listening to us when we say such things as, "Wow, do you know what I discovered? This is so interesting!"

We could introduce our kids to words such as 'force', 'friction', 'gravity' and 'energy' while sharing our observations. How about telling a few stories? My kids love hearing about the time, many years ago, when I climbed to the top of a tall and rickety metal slippery dip. It was a long way down. Was I brave enough to let go of the safety rail? I sat down, shuffled forward, and then gravity took over. I slid down and down and then shot off the end of the slippery dip, landing on the grass. I stood up, a grin on my face. The thrill of the descent was worth the burning sensation in my legs: it was a hot summer's day, and the sun's energy had passed into the metal slide before moving into my skin!

So we can ponder, wonder, tell stories, and share our observations with our fellow explorers. But we shouldn't take over and make our kids listen to us or bombard them with questions that we expect them to answer. If we do that, we might stifle their curiosity and lose their trust. We must be sensitive to how much information our kids are looking for and not be tempted to turn every moment into a lecture.

It seems to me that kids learn best when they have lots of free time to explore and experiment, try things out and see what happens. What do you think?

The Challenge

1. Observe your kids interacting with the world around them.

2. Think about what they're experiencing.

3. Be a fellow curious explorer.

4. Make some notes about the learning you discover.

I'm sure you'll be surprised how much your kids are learning while playing or doing 'nothing much at all'.

5. You could transfer these learning notes to your homeschool records book!

Related Reading

The Curriculum of Life: Curious Unschoolers

How to Get Our Children to Trust Us: Curious Unschoolers

18. Discover Your Talents

We all have talents, don't we? We could have artistic, musical, or academic talents. We may have organisational ones like Marie Kondo! Perhaps we have excellent communication skills or love to keep our heads busy solving problems. Or we could be naturally gentle, patient, sensitive or interested in other people.

Even though we all have talents, perhaps some of us haven't yet discovered what they are. Could our school experiences have prevented us from exploring our interests and finding the areas where we excel? Or maybe we were discouraged from using our talents and following our passions.

As a child, I loved writing stories and dreamed of becoming an author. I'd compose stories in my head when I was in bed before I went to sleep. I had a cardboard grocery box of half-written stories about princesses and large families similar to the Brady Bunch. I imagined my books filed under S on a library shelf and wished that my surname wasn't Skeleton but something that started with a letter further up the alphabet. I was sure not many people made it all the way to the library aisles containing the books written by authors with names R-Z.

Despite my passion for writing, during my teenage years, my dream faded away. I was too busy doing schoolwork - assignments and exams - to write stories. Also, being an author seemed impossible. People told me only a few writers successfully publish books. I thought I wasn't one of them because no one encouraged me, saying my work could be good enough. So, instead of writing, I found myself doing a science degree because this was regarded as an excellent career choice. Although I'm fascinated by how our world works, I didn't enjoy my science degree or working in that industry.

One day, when I was a younger mother, I was asked to write an article for a homeschool newsletter. (The editor always needed help to get enough contributions.) At first, I protested: "I've got nothing to write about!" I thought I couldn't do it. But after some firm encouragement - the deadline for the next edition was fast approaching - I gave it a go. And I rediscovered my enjoyment of writing.

Later, I got into blogging and writing books because of someone's encouraging words. After our son Thomas died, I wrote an article for our homeschool newsletter about him, and Fr James Tierney (author of the *Bush Boys* books) suggested I write a book about the experience of losing a baby. Later, he encouraged me to write children's novels. Fr Jim became my writing buddy, and we began beta reading and promoting each other's books.

An interest of mine that didn't appear until adulthood is public speaking. As a child, I had to give a speech in front of the class every term. I found this torturous. Standing before my fellow students, I'd shake and turn red. It was awful! I thought it was cruel to push kids to do such things. Nowadays, I enjoy talking to groups of people though most of my speaking at the moment is in front of a camera. I've concluded that pushing kids to do what they find difficult isn't helpful. Maybe we need time and space to discover our talents without any pressure. And once we find out what we enjoy doing, some encouraging words help us pursue our dreams.

The Challenge

1. Scribble down some answers to these questions:

What are your talents? Did you experience the right conditions as a child for them to appear? Or did you discover your talents as an adult? Or maybe you're still searching for the things you're good at because you still haven't had an opportunity to explore, experiment and discover where your talents lie?

When you were a child, were your talents encouraged? Did someone tell you to dream big?

Or were you discouraged from pursuing the interests that excited you? Were you told you'd never make a career out of them? Were the important things to you labelled as 'spare time' interests? Perhaps you were only allowed to do them after you'd completed the work other people thought was more important?

How does using your talents make you feel? Do your passions bring you joy? Do they take you to your happy place?

How could you use your talents today? Should you use them? Could you improve them? Is it time to do something you've always wanted to do?

Do your experiences affect the way you look at your kids' talents? Should you encourage your children to do the things that bring them alive? Or do you need to step back and not pressure them to use their talents in the way you think is best?

2. Find ways to use your talents and let your kids use theirs.

It's important. Talents are part of who we are. When we use them, we become more fully alive. They bring us joy.

Related Reading

Helping a Child Discover Her Talents: Curious Unschoolers

Do Our Passions Complete Us as People?: Curious Unschoolers

19: Have an Engaging Conversation

Imogen, Gemma-Rose and I had some wonderful conversations while on a 9-hour (each way) road trip to see my daughter Sophie. Imogen was our driver, Gemma-Rose was in charge of our music, and I had nothing to do but enjoy the journey.

After asking for our music suggestions, Gemma-Rose put together a playlist of songs for our listening pleasure. Then we sang along, danced in our seats and chatted about each track. Many of the songs were from my younger days. Listening to one of them, I said, "I first heard this song at a disco. Dad and I used to go dancing every Saturday night. I had a short white dress with gold threads woven into the fabric. I had gold boots too. And you should have seen my makeup." I mentioned vinyl record albums, record players, and computers that filled a room. My daughters soaked up my stories of being young in a different era. One story led to another, and we found ourselves discussing all kinds of fascinating topics.

Another time, Gemma-Rose and I had an interesting conversation that began while looking at movie-themed jewellery online. We chatted about superheroes, the strange names some parents choose for their children, movie versions of books, and musicals. Somehow we arrived at *Les Miserables*. I said, "I never got around to watching the movie version," and Gemma-Rose said, "Nor did I." Then we turned on the TV and watched it together. And we continued talking.

It doesn't matter what we talk about, does it? Every topic is potentially interesting. We can always find an angle into a subject that will capture our attention.

We learn a lot by talking together, don't we? We swap information, share opinions, ponder thoughts and ideas, find solutions to problems and tell stories while having an enjoyable time.

We also learn to listen carefully as we take an interest in what other people say, valuing their input. We recognise the importance of taking turns and including everyone in the conversation. We learn to communicate effectively by talking respectfully and generously with other people.

Sometimes it's hard to listen rather than talk. We may be tempted to use a conversation to lecture our kids, telling them what they should believe and what we think they should know. But, if we can resist the urge to do this and instead listen to them, we can learn a lot about their thoughts, ideas, and opinions. We could learn something very valuable.

So, conversations lead to lots of learning. And they can be a source of delight, wonder, fun, enjoyment and connection.

The Challenge

1. Begin a conversation.

Where will you talk? Around the dinner table? While walking a dog? In the car? During a one-on-one time with a child?

2. Ensure everyone has a chance to talk.

3. Accept everyone's points of view.

Our conversations can be lively, but we want them to be free of arguments.

4. Enjoy!

5. Later, write down the main points of the conversation.

Are there any ideas you want to follow up? Did you mention any books or movies you could strew? Did you talk about anything you could label English, Creative Arts or History? Can you add a few notes to your homeschool records book?

6. Open up regular opportunities for conversations.

Invite your kids to walk with you or have morning tea at a cafe. You could eat dinner or lunch together at the table. How about having a family dinner party?

7. Improve your own conversation skills.

Years ago, Andy and I did an art of conversation course. Every Saturday afternoon for a couple of months, we gathered together with other parents, eager to learn how to communicate with each other better. I'm sure, at first, we all thought we were excellent conversationalists. Didn't we talk to each other all the time? We had no shortage of words. But we soon discovered we had a lot to learn.

It's not okay to talk over the top of each other. What about the quiet person who'd like to join in but can't find an opportunity? How about our habit of continually directing the conversation towards topics we want to discuss? Should we take an interest in other people's ideas and thoughts instead of imposing ours on everyone else?

Doing an art of conversation course or reading a book on this topic is beneficial, but we can always practice our skills by talking with our families. And then our kids learn how to communicate effectively too.

Often, people ask homeschoolers this question: "What about socialisation?" What do they mean by the word 'socialisation'? Why are they so anxious that our kids socialise? Do they think our kids won't be able to effectively communicate with a range of people when they go out into the bigger world?

People may label homeschoolers weird and unsociable, but my children have no difficulty talking to others, including those who are different from them. They have good communication skills. And this is something not all kids have.

"They don't know how to talk properly," observed Sophie referring to some school kids she knows. "They have no idea how to have proper conversations where everyone is included. They talk about themselves all the time. They're not interested in hearing what other people have to say. They don't really want to know about me."

And this can be hard. How do you become part of the conversation when no one is willing to listen and is uninterested in what you might have to say? When nobody even realises you'd like them to include you? Often, my girls give up. As they say, sometimes it's the people who are always speaking who have a problem. Just because someone has no shortage of words doesn't mean she knows how to talk.

Getting together regularly with other people doesn't necessarily teach us how to communicate and get on with others. That's the conclusion I came to. I stopped worrying about such things as homeschool groups and organised field trips. As long as kids are capable of being sociable, it doesn't matter if they choose to stay home.

Yes, our kids learn to communicate effectively within our families as long as we have conversations with them and obey the conversation 'rules'.

Related Reading

Making Friends and Being Different: Radical Unschool Love

20: Give Joyful Praise

My daughter Imogen sings the last note, and a big silly grin appears on my face as I applaud loudly with the rest of the concert audience. Imogen smiles with delight and retreats to the side of the stage.

Later, on our way home, I say, "Oh wow! You sang beautifully. Those high notes sent shivers up my spine. I really enjoyed your performance. I'm sure you brought joy to a lot of people's lives tonight."

And listening to my praise, my daughter's heart floods with joy as well.

Joy: that's what I think praise is all about. It originates from joy and results in joy. And what could be wrong with that?

Unfortunately, many people, including parenting experts and some unschoolers, disagree with my understanding of praise and warn us of its dangers. They tell us to stay well away from it because it's manipulative: it encourages kids only to do the things that please us. Without praise, they won't be motivated to work hard and become the people they were created to be. It could make kids think they're better than everyone else.

Years ago, I read these opinions, but they didn't match up to my experiences with my children. I wondered what I should do. What if the experts are right? Perhaps I should stop praising and become a 'proper' unschooler and responsible mother. Or could I continue praising my kids but not tell anyone so no one would think I was a bad parent? I decided to do something completely different: I started talking about my reasons for praising and now encourage others to do something that brings a lot of joy to both child and parent.

Is praise manipulative?

There is no doubt that praise does encourage us to do particular things, but what if instead of it pushing us to become the people others think we should be, it reassures us that we're okay as we are? What if it tells us that what we want to do is important and that we should continue doing the things that matter to us? There's no need to change to please anyone. People believe in us, accept us, and trust us. They love us unconditionally.

My kids sometimes say they're proud of me. They did this when I decided to become a runner. Even though I limped home after my first run, convinced I was about to die, my girls thought I was wonderful. I was brave and willing to endure the pain. I could do this. They were right: after hearing my kids' praise, I knew I couldn't give up. I continued running.

When I finished writing my first two unschooling books, a couple of friends and my sister said they were proud of me too. Their words warmed my heart, filling it with joy. Their praise gave my dreams wings. I thought: *Because people believe in me, I can do anything*. I rushed off to work on another book. And here it is!

To be sincere and effective when praising our kids, we must know them well. We can't just toss out a few familiar words - "Well done! You're a great person!" - and hope that will do. Oh no, praising is much more difficult than that. Of course, I don't have to know my favourite barista well before praising his coffee-making skill. When I thank him and give him some positive feedback, which I often do, I only have to know the difference between a good coffee and a bad one!

What if praise tells us our parents feel joy because we're part of their lives?

There are times when joy washes over us unexpectedly. We look at our children with full hearts. Are we really the parents of these beautiful people? It would be hard not to let that joy spill over and become "I'm so proud of you!"

Why hold those words back? We have to say them because our children need to hear them.

Why not praise and bring so much joy to our kids and ourselves?

The Challenge

1. Connect closely with your kids. Observe them, so you see how unique and wonderfully made they are.

2. Be grateful for your children.

3. When you feel joy wash through your heart, let words of praise fall from your lips.

4. Tell your kids they bring you joy.

5. Feel the joy of passing on joy!

6. Make sure your kids know they're okay. Be specific with your praise. Tell your kids you believe in them. You trust them. Your words will give wings to their dreams!

An Extra Challenge

Watch out for opportunities to praise people from outside your family. For example, you could thank your barista for your excellent cup of coffee. Maybe his eyes will light up at your words. He could say, "Not many people take the time to give positive feedback on their coffee. You've made my day!"

Related Reading

The Beginning and End of Praise: Radical Unschool Love

Why I Am My Kids' Number One Fan: Radical Unschool Love

21: Be a Maths Detective

"We use maths all the time."

"Kids will learn maths because they need it for everyday life."

Have you ever heard people say these things, but you haven't been convinced? Perhaps the problem is that, although maths surrounds us, we fail to see it. We don't look properly. But once we put on our maths eyes, it's obvious that maths is everywhere!

Years ago, when my girls and I started running together, we wondered how far it was around the playing fields. How far were we running each day? We wanted to know.

At that time, we didn't have GPS trackers or phones that we could use to calculate the distance, so we borrowed a measuring wheel from Andy's primary school. We then pushed it around the field's perimeter and discovered it was 500 m or 0.5 km.

500 m? That was perfect. An easy-to-work-with number! We then knew we needed to run ten laps of the field if we wanted to go 5 km.

A while after we did our measuring, the council moved one side of the playing field fence, increasing the field's area. Of course, moving the fence affected the perimeter of the field. Fortunately, I had bought a GPS tracker by that time, so we used it to determine the new distance. It was 520 m.

The other day, my daughter Charlotte and I took our dogs for a walk through the bush. We headed down a track that runs close to the back of our house, and soon we could see our garden fence.

"This was the bush that was back-burnt during the bushfire," I said. (The blackened trees that surrounded us made my words unnecessary.) The fire was only a short distance from our home. "How far do you think it is between the burnt bush and our garden?"

We estimated 50 m or less. Then I pointed to a tree along the track that was slightly further away from us than our garden fence. "Let's measure the distance to that tree using my GPS tracker."

We walked back along the track for 50 m and arrived at the tree. That meant the bushfire had been burning less than 50 m from our garden. That's not far, is it?

"It's just as well we had lots of firefighters and the water bombing helicopters controlling the fire," I said. And then we relived those frightening but strangely exciting hours when we'd stood in our garden watching the helicopters swooping low over our house, thick smoke billowing from the bush. Sirens sounded as the water fell upon the flames. Then the helicopters rose and returned to the dam to refill their tanks. And we captured the action on our phones, wondering if it would be wiser to prepare to evacuate our home. But there was no need to panic. Although the fire was less than 50 m away, the firefighters and helicopter pilots did a magnificent job of controlling it.

You might not like running. Perhaps you've never experienced a bushfire. But I'm sure you have encountered maths in loads of situations. It's there in the ordinary events of our lives as well as the extraordinary ones.

The Challenge

You can do this challenge alone or invite your kids to join you. You could say, "Does anyone want to be a maths detective?"

1. Put on your maths eyes and look carefully.

2. Make a list of all the maths you discover.

3. Take some photos. They'll be useful for your homeschool records books.

4. If you find someone using maths, you get extra points!

Maybe these ideas will get you started:

- Do you measure out food for a dog or cat?

- What size cartons of milk do you buy?

- Do you have a calendar on your wall?

- Or a clock?

- Or perhaps you use the digital clock on your microwave.

- What 2D and 3D shapes can you see?

- Do you have tessellated tiles on your kitchen walls or the floor?

- Can you see any examples of symmetry?

- How about the numbers on a phone, coins, clothes tags, Kindle e-books, and grocery receipts?

- Is there any maths in a junk mail catalogue, sheet music, a recipe book or on a breakfast cereal box?

- When you're away from home, will you discover maths on signs displaying shop opening hours or fuel prices? How about car dashboards and road signs? Of course, you'll find loads of maths in a supermarket!

5. If any of your maths discoveries lead to interesting conversations or set you off on rabbit trails, make notes about what you discuss and find out. You might be surprised how much learning you and your kids end up doing!

Related Reading

Becoming Real-Life Maths Detectives: Curious Unschoolers

22: Say Thank you to Your Kids

Should we say thank you more often?

We always make a point of showing appreciation to people from outside our families. If our friends do something for us, we make sure we say thank you. But do we always remember to thank our children, our husbands, and our wives for the things they do for us? For example, the chores.

Do we say, "Thank you for cleaning my bathroom"? Or do we treat that chore as something that's run of the mill, something our children have to do? We might believe it's their duty to perform these tasks, so we don't see the need to thank them. Chores are just part of the work of the family. We shouldn't have to thank each other for the things that we're doing.

However, thank yous make life go more smoothly: they oil our interactions with others. It's also good to know that people appreciate our efforts, isn't it? Even if we must do something, it does make it a lot easier and more rewarding if somebody notices what we're doing. Our words can also bring joy to others. We should, especially, bring that joy to our own families.

We can also say thank you for things other than chores.

"Thank you for watching that video with me. I enjoyed spending time with you."

"Thank you for cooking the dinner. It was delicious."

"Thank you for taking the dog for a walk. I didn't feel like going out today. I'm tired."

"Thank you for chatting with me. I enjoyed our conversation."

"Thank you for listening. I felt like talking about that with somebody today."

"Thank you for the hug. It was beautiful. You give the best hugs."

The Challenge

1. Watch out for opportunities to say thank you to your family.

2. Express your thanks in a visible way.

Isn't it wonderful when someone gives us a bunch of thank you flowers, a box of chocolates, or a huge hug?

Could you arrange a little thank you gift for your children? Will their eyes light up if you do that? How wide will they grin? Will their smiles be as big as yours? Joy is contagious, isn't it?

23: Strew the School Subjects

Strewing is an integral part of unschooling. We're constantly looking for resources that might enrich our kids' lives by introducing them to new ideas, skills or knowledge. Or we could strew things related to the interests of our children. We hope to enhance their learning experiences.

I used to enjoy searching for resources. On a quiet afternoon, I'd often open up my laptop and begin googling such things as 'real life maths', 'art history resources' or 'best history documentaries'. If I discovered any exciting resources, I'd add them to our strewing notebook. Then I'd say in a casual kind of way, "I've added some links to some interesting videos... or books ... or websites to our notebook. I think you'll like the art ones. Why not take a look?"

But, of course, we can strew real things as well as digital links. Years ago, I used to do this before we got a computer and the Internet. Gradually, I built up a collection of non-fiction and fiction print books, CDs, DVDs, art and craft materials, writing materials, science kits and games. We ended up with so much stuff piled on bookshelves and in cupboards that we sometimes forgot what we owned.

One day, at the start of a new school year, I decided we had enough resources in our home: we didn't need to buy anything else. So, I set myself a challenge. Could I find at least one resource for each traditional school subject? Perhaps I could strew something that might spark my children's interest. They might end up learning about something the educational department had decided they should know. More importantly, they might discover some new passions. I hoped my kids would get excited by such things as Australian poetry by Henry Lawson, Shakespeare's *Macbeth*, and *The Nutcracker* ballet. Maybe they'd want to sew a few sock dolls, experiment with some kitchen science, take a few photos and hear about some daring Australian bushrangers.

So, while my school teacher husband spent hours preparing lesson plans for his class, I strolled around our house with a basket, searching shelves and looking into cupboards and drawers. Thirty minutes later, my basket was full of DVDs, CDs, books, science sets, games and odds and ends such as a compass, paper dolls, and a pile of old socks. I felt excited. I hoped my kids would feel the same way.

When I'd finished my strewing, I looked at my husband, who still had his head bent over his computer, and I felt grateful we were unschoolers.

The Challenge

Find one resource for each of the subjects your children would be studying if they were in school: English, Maths, Science, Geography, History, Creative Arts, Personal Development, Health and Physical Education.

You could find a game such as Uno, Monopoly, chess or sudoku that uses maths. How about a maths colouring book? Or a junk mail catalogue? A set of scales? A board game that needs dice?

You could grab a couple of your favourite childhood novels off the bookshelf for English. Or do you have an empty journal or a diary stashed away somewhere? Or perhaps one written by a famous person? Do you have a Shakespeare or Jane Austen DVD? How about some picture books? Or some magnetic letters?

Can you find a compass, map, travel DVD, postcards or stamps that could be geography resources?

A magnifying glass, science kit, pine cone, packet of seeds, thermometer, prism, and a rock or two might spark an interest in science.

A family heirloom, photo album, period drama movie, war medal, and some historical fiction novels could represent history.

Some paint and a potato, a polaroid camera, a paper-making kit, a ballet DVD and some ballerina paper dolls, a triangle or set of bells, a print of a famous painting, and cake decorating supplies could all lead to some creative arts.

For personal development, health and physical education, you could find a ball, a piece of elastic for playground games, some chalk for hopscotch, a DVD such as *Chariots of Fire*, a religious medal, a Bible, or a prayer.

The possibilities are endless!

The Challenge 'Rules'

1. Find at least one resource for each learning area.

2. Collect only resources you find in your home. Don't buy anything. Don't use anything digital.

3. Strew the resources in a place where your children will see them: a table, basket or kitchen bench.

4. It's okay to invite your children to use your resources:

"Would you like to watch this movie with me?"

"We could take some photos together."

"How about we read this book together? I read this when I was a child."

It would help if you remain detached. Let your children accept or ignore the resource suggestions. After a few days, you could replace the rejected things and try again.

5. If the resources excite you, but your children aren't interested, you can use them yourself.

You never know what might happen if your children see you watching a nature documentary or planting sunflower seeds. "What are you doing, Mum? Can I do that too?" Yes, they might want to join in!

6. In your homeschool records book, list the resources your kids used, add the appropriate school subject labels, and write down some notes about any learning adventures.

I hope this challenge will show you that kids can learn maths, English, science and all the traditional school subjects just by using things you already have in your home. You don't need to buy a curriculum or expensive resources.

Of course, all of us do buy things from time to time. Maybe while doing this challenge, you might find a few things you bought a long time ago and have yet to use.

Challenging ourselves not to buy anything reminds me of a time when I loved stocking up on resources. There were certain things I thought I just had to have. My kids' education wouldn't be complete if I didn't buy them. So I parted with my money and brought more stuff home, which ended up unused on shelves. Yes, I discovered that 'essential' turned into 'not needed' very quickly.

During a brief classical homeschooling stage, I searched high and low for a set of *The Great Books of the Western World.* I grinned when I found a pristine set, pages never opened, in a secondhand bookshop. I brought the books home and displayed them on a shelf in our living room. And for years, that's where they've remained. We've never opened them.

Curricula has never tempted me, but right back at the beginning, before my oldest kids even reached school age, I thought I needed to buy a set of encyclopedias. They were essential if my kids were to have a good education.

Good Education

When I open the front door, a man with a winning smile immediately launches into a slick presentation. Do I have children? Yes, I have two. Would I like them to receive a good education? Yes. Do I want to give them the best start in life? Of course. It's my lucky day. The young man tells me he has just what I need: a set of encyclopaedias.

He thrusts a brochure at me and says he can give me a special deal. I tell him it all sounds good, but I'm not going to buy anything without first speaking to my husband. The winning smile wavers. What time will my husband be home? 6 pm? The salesman will return at the appropriate hour.

Later, the man appears again on our doorstep with some samples of his books, and he spends a long time telling us how magnificent they are. The encyclopaedia set isn't cheap. But that's okay because the salesman has a plan. We can pay for the books in instalments. It will be worth it. Money well spent. An investment. We don't want to deny our kids a fabulous education, do we?

Andy and I like the look of the books. They're crammed with information. And they come with lots of extras: reading plans, dictionaries and a special guide for kids. If we have a question, the encyclopaedia can answer it. It could be our kids' passport to the world.

Although we're interested, we don't want to make a rushed decision. Can we think about it? A frown replaces his smile as the salesman steps up his game. The special offer won't last very long. Surely we don't want to miss out? But we're firm. We're not going to buy the set without discussing it first.

Once the salesman has gone, we do some encyclopaedia maths. We look at Andy's wage and all our bills. How much money do we have left over at the end of each month? It doesn't take us long to realise that we can't afford to give our kids a good education.

So, we don't have a long row of large, red, glossy books with gold-edged information-packed pages sitting on our shelf. Our kids aren't soaking up all those A-Z entries. I feel rather sad about this for a time. But then the salesman's words fade, and I regain my commonsense.

A good education isn't packed neatly inside an encyclopaedia. Every time we open a page, we get a taste, a bite or two of knowledge. But learning is much bigger than a set of books. It's more magnificent and exciting and interesting.

We can find learning in everything we see, hear, touch, smell and taste. It's in the movies we watch, the stories we read, the places we go, the conversations we have, the joys and sorrows we feel, the challenges and failures and triumphs we face, the thoughts and ideas we ponder, the everyday things we do together, the relationships and connections we share, and everything else we experience in our lives.

These days, probably no one buys encyclopaedias, but parents do buy curricula, sometimes many, hoping that one day, they'll discover one that contains everything their child needs to know. Learning all packaged neatly into a number of pages, a box, a set of computer files. Organised and labelled. Assessment included. A perfect education.

Does that sound tempting?

Or would you rather have the world?

24: Ponder Trust

Do you have a firm belief in unschooling? Are you sure your unschooled kids will become the people they are meant to be? Will they learn all they need to know to live happy and successful lives?

Can you trust unschooling? Do you trust your kids? How about yourself?

If you have already done the *Explore Screen Time* challenge, you'll know exactly what to do for this next one. Instead of writing about screen time and devices, you're going to write about another big topic that could be a stumbling block for unschooling: trust.

The Challenge

1. Find a pen and paper or open your device.

2. Set a timer for ten minutes.

3. Free write about trust, pouring your thoughts onto the page or screen without stopping.

Here are some questions you might like to ponder:

What is trust? How could you build trust between yourself and your kids? Do you have to be trustworthy? What gets in the way of trust? How does trusting make you feel? Scared? What will happen if you don't trust? How does it feel not to be trusted?

Do you have any trust stories you could write about? Have you allowed your kids to do something that required trust? Or maybe you've found it impossible to trust?

Are you finding it hard to trust that your kids will learn all they need to know by unschooling?

Were you trusted when you were a child? Do you trust yourself? Or do you doubt you can do what you want to do? Do you worry about other people's opinions? Do you listen to them because, while you were growing up, people - parents and teachers - said they knew better than you?

What would you do, and how would you feel if you did trust yourself? What if you could do the work you have the talent and yearning to do without worrying about what others might say about your efforts? What if you could make the choices that, deep down, you know are right for you?

Can you provide your kids with something other people might have denied you? Can you give them the gift of trust? With it, would they feel confident and comfortable with who they are? Would they be more likely to give things a go without worrying about possible failure and criticism? Would your kids live fully, not ruled by the opinions of others? Would they be free of the self-doubt many of us battle as we try to do what we feel called to do?

4. Read what you've written.

Have you discovered an idea or thought worth exploring in more depth?

5. Take that idea or thought and free write about it for another ten minutes.

6. Did you discover anything new about trust? Make some notes about your thoughts.

Trust is complicated, isn't it? As you can see from my questions, we could approach it from many angles. You could do this challenge multiple times, focusing on different questions each time.

Here's something that I wrote about trust:

Can kids be trusted? If we give them the freedom to direct their lives, won't they do nothing much at all? Won't they choose to be lazy?

I wonder if we have trouble trusting our kids because we remember what we were like when we were children. Perhaps we weren't keen to work hard. Could we have spent lots of time avoiding such things as chores? Maybe we weren't dedicated to our school work and needed someone to push us along so that we completed our assignments.

Could our experiences have convinced us that it wouldn't be sensible to let go of control? Kids need motivating. Without us, they won't work.

But our kids aren't us. Their experiences and ours are very different. We probably never had a chance to set our own challenges. We weren't allowed to follow our interests. Instead, we had to do what our parents and teachers decided was best for us. We had to fulfil other people's expectations. And so we lost our inborn drive to work. Why show interest when we have no control?

I don't give my kids the impression that I don't trust them to work hard. Oh no, I have complete confidence in them, which is just as well because if I didn't, my kids would become reliant on me. If I don't give them their freedom, they'll end up like I was as a child: they'll only work when other people push them.

Our kids have something else that encourages them to work hard: our good example. But what if we are still reluctant to work? That's not a good example to follow, is it? Well, most parents can't choose to be lazy. Family life involves lots of sacrifices. That's just the way it is. So, our kids observe us giving up our time for them, putting them ahead of ourselves, and working hard (without complaining!).

Of course, there are still times when we can choose to work or not. These occasions increase as our kids get older. Sometimes when I have a choice, I'm tempted to be lazy and selfish. I want only to do the things I enjoy. I want to use my status as a mother to avoid the more unpleasant work of the family. I'd like to leave the things I don't want to do to someone else. But I don't. Because how can I treat the people I love the most like that?

Love is a powerful motivator, isn't it? It can push us to do difficult things we might not want to do. It can change us all.

An Extra Challenge

If you'd like to explore trust from a faith perspective, you could ponder the following questions:

How can we expect to let go of control of our kids' lives if we can't let go of control of our own?

Why do we want to be in control? Do we think we know better than God? Don't we trust Him?

What do we want our lives to look like? Do we hope our days will be happy and problem-free? Are we afraid we might have to suffer if we entrust our lives to God?

Will suffering arrive whether we want it to or not? Is it impossible to erect a barrier to protect ourselves from it? Will it happen to everyone? Is it part of life?

Can we deal with suffering on our own? Or do we need God? We can't just call upon God when things get difficult, can we?

What do we think giving our lives to God looks like? Does it involve praying? Trying to be the person God created us to be? Living by the commandments? Is that enough? Or do we also need to accept everything God allows in our lives? For example, I used to think that if I prayed a lot and tried to avoid sin, that was enough. If I were a good Christian, God would protect me from difficulties. I wouldn't need to trust.

Why should we let go of control of our kids' lives? How do we know what they will need when we can't predict the future? Should we entrust our kids' lives to God because He has a plan for each of them?

Should we make a few plans, glancing towards the future but be aware the result isn't all about us? Should we live in the moment, attending to what's happening right now? Should we be willing for things to turn out differently from our plans?

Related Reading

All About Trust: Radical Unschool Love

Unschooling and Trust: Curious Unschoolers

25: Turn No into Yes

As I walked into the supermarket ahead of my daughter Charlotte, she stopped and said, "Wait!" She waved a hand towards the flower display next to the shop entrance. "I'd like to buy you some flowers. Which ones would you like?"

A smile spread across my face as I looked at the roses, chrysanthemums, daisies, and proteas, trying to decide what I'd like. Perhaps I should choose the least expensive ones? "No, Mum, I want to buy you the flowers you like best!"

I came home with a beautiful bouquet, an unexpected gift I enjoy every time I look towards the place I've put my vase: the coffee table in front of the sofa, my favourite place to sit.

When my kids were younger, sometimes I'd notice them looking at something on a shop shelf, and I'd say, "Which one would you like to take home?" Or I'd see things while shopping by myself and think, "Sophie... Gemma-Rose... Callum... would love that!" I'd buy it, bring it home and give it to the appropriate child.

Maybe we get worried about spoiling our kids. Should we be careful what we give them because they might expect something every time we go shopping? And what if we have more than one child? If we buy something for one of them, will we have to buy something for everyone? That's only fair, isn't it?

Despite the warnings, I still bought gifts for no reason except to spread joy. And nothing terrible happened. Being generous never led to my kids begging for more whenever we went shopping. They always appreciated whatever I gave them. The child who received a gift would smile with delight. And those who didn't get anything were happy too. They'd share in the joy.

It's good when we are happy for each other. When we don't compare and keep a balance sheet and worry about fairness. And it's wonderful when someone wants to visibly show their love for us.

I still buy unexpected gifts: a bag of nuts, a book, a bottle of nail polish, or even a tiny Freddy Frog or Caramello Koala. These days, I place my gifts on the appropriate person's pillow and wait for my family to discover them when they return home from work. Pillow presents have become 'my thing', a way to say, "I thought of you today. I love you so very much."

Now and then, I stop writing this story and glance up at my flowers; joy fills my heart. I feel very loved indeed.

Our kids learn so much from us, don't they? Will they learn to be afraid? Or will they follow our example, ignore the warnings, and do things that might not seem sensible to most people? Will they spread joy and show their love? Will our kids do this because we choose to parent them without fear?

Will they, like us, turn no into yes?

There are many situations where we could say no to our kids instead of yes, aren't there? Sometimes no ends up being our default answer to most of our kids' requests. But is it sometimes okay to say yes? In this challenge, we'll explore these questions!

The Challenge

1. List the reasons why you say no when your kids are hoping you'll say yes.

You might say no to a dog because a pet involves a lot of work.

If your child dyes her hair blue, you could be concerned about what people might say.

Perhaps you're not willing or unable to make time to help your children with activities such as baking.

Painting involves a mess you might have to clean up, so will you say no?

What if your teens want to spend time with their friends? Where will they go? What will they do? Will you worry if you say yes?

How about climbing trees? Will a no keep your children safe from injury?

2. Examine your reasons and decide whether they're valid.

Is a no in the best interests of your child? Or does a no benefit you?

Maybe we sometimes say no to protect our parenting reputation. What will people think if we allow our kids to dye their hair blue, play video games all day, and watch particular movies? Is a parent who can stick firmly to her no a good parent? Or maybe not?

What if we buy things because our kids might like them and we want to create joy? Will we end up spoiling our children? They may get used to getting what they want and always expect to get their own way. Will they become greedy and self-centred, not caring about other people?

Do kids learn about self-denial when we force them to go without?

"I won't give my kids much, so they learn to appreciate what they have."

"My kids have lots of toys, so I'm going to donate most of my Christmas money to a charity instead of buying them gifts."

Or is self-sacrifice something kids have to choose for themselves? Does it have to come from within? Will they be motivated to put others first, be generous with their time, money and possessions, and turn a no into a yes for someone else by experiencing this for themselves? Is our self-giving example important? Because, of course, we can't expect our kids to do anything we're unwilling to do. And do our close connections allow us to discuss such things, which might be more productive than inferring our kids are greedy and should change their ways?

Do we choose no thinking this response will protect our kids, keeping them safe? Or does a no protect us, the parents, rather than our children? Because sometimes, when we say no, we don't have to step outside our comfort zone. We don't have to trust our kids. We eliminate worry. But how will our kids grow and develop if we think only of ourselves and our feelings?

What if our kids really do need things? Should we say no, refuse to buy them, forcing them to work to get them? We might be scared to say yes because we're afraid our children will become lazy. We make things unnecessarily difficult for them by saying no and putting too many obstacles in their way when we're supposed to be helping them rather than frustrating them.

3. Look for a way to turn a no into a yes.

You might be reluctant to let your kids ride their bikes on the road. What if they get hit by a car? So, to keep your kids safe and to prevent you from worrying, you could confine their bike riding to places such as your garden. But what if you arrange for someone to teach your kids road skills? Are there any bike safety courses? Could you accompany your kids on their rides until they're confident in traffic? Could they learn the skills needed to turn a no into a yes?

Do the advantages of owning and looking after a dog outweigh the work? If cost is a problem, how about choosing a small dog from a rescue centre? Or you could get a cat. Would a mouse work? Or is the idea of a dog suddenly more attractive than a rodent?

It's okay to give kids things that they don't necessarily need. Joy is a good reason for saying yes. Joy for our child and joy for us. Doesn't God delight in our delight when He generously gives us more than we need?

It can be hard to ignore other people's opinions, but are our kids more important than our parental reputation? We shouldn't worry about such things as clothes and blue hair. If anyone frowns, is their friendship worth keeping?

It's okay to give our kids whatever they need. If we do that, will they follow our example in the future when we are old and in need of help ourselves? Or when that time comes, will our kids say, "You should have worked hard to prepare for your retirement? You can't expect me to help. I have to put myself first. I have my own life to live."

Could trying not to spoil our kids actually teach them to be self-centred? What do you think?

An Extra Challenge

Looking at this challenge slightly differently, could we turn a no into a yes for ourselves?

Could we say yes, we're willing to be more adventurous and try new things? Perhaps we sit on the sidelines of life, too afraid to do particular activities because we think we might fail. What if we embarrass ourselves? But what are we missing out on while we're telling ourselves no?

Could we say yes, we're willing to put aside our fears and trust? Trust ourselves. Trust our kids. Trust God. Are we missing out on something good because we're hanging on tightly, unwilling to give up control? Do we need to give ourselves permission to relax and let go? It can be exhausting trying to hold everything together. It may be okay if we don't.

Related Reading

Saying Yes: Radical Unschool Love

Are Your Young Adult Kids Still Living at Home?: Radical Unschool Love

Being Brave, Adventurous and Just a Bit Daring: Radical Unschool Love

Saying No: Radical Unschool Love

Sometimes We Don't Need a Good Reason: Radical Unschool Love

26: Compose an Elevator Pitch

A few years ago, I was listening to a podcast while running, and the hosts began discussing why they are Catholic. What would they say if they only had a very short time to tell someone what draws them to the Catholic faith? What would their 'elevator pitch' be?

My mind wandered away from the podcast as I thought about my own elevator pitch. If the person next to me in the elevator suddenly said, "You're wearing a crucifix. Why are you a Catholic?", could I give my reasons before we reached the top floor?

Before I'd composed my pitch in my mind using only a few perfect sentences, I started thinking about unschooling. We often have to explain our way of life quickly, don't we? And often, we get tongue-tied while trying to tell someone precisely what unschooling is. There are times when we avoid talking about what we do. It's just too difficult. Perhaps no one will understand. People might think we're crazy. But what if we have an elevator pitch ready for those moments? Instead of brushing the subject away, we could confidently explain unschooling and why it's important to us. Our elevator pitches might intrigue the people we're talking with, and maybe they'll want to know more.

Also, elevator pitches can remind us why we're unschooling. When we're having a wobbly moment and start to doubt what we're doing, we can give the pitch to ourselves!

The Challenge

1. Write down your reasons for unschooling. If you haven't fully embraced unschooling, write down what you're doing now and why.

Write quickly without worrying about producing the perfect words. You could free write. This exercise could double up as a writing challenge!

2. When you have jotted down all your reasons, prune, reorganise and change your words until you have a clear paragraph or two that you're happy with.

3. Watch out for opportunities - at the shops, homeschooling meetings, and family gatherings - where you could share your pitches.

Of course, our words shouldn't be defensive, attacking or critical of other people. Finding the perfect words could be a challenge of its own!

27: See Kids as They Really Are

Babies are gorgeous, aren't they? With their soft newborn skin, little fingers that curl around ours, that unique baby scent and eyes which search for ours, they make our hearts flutter with love.

I'm sure you remember the first time you met each of your children. Weren't those magical moments? We probably all thought our babies were absolutely perfect. But do we still feel that way now that our babies have grown older?

In my story *Perfectly Them*, I wrote:

It's very sad that initial impressions wear off. We begin to see faults in our children. As they grow, we criticise and complain. Perhaps that's because we wonder how they're going to get on in life and fit into the world. If only they were different.

Maybe we justify our negative words. Surely it's our duty to point out our children's faults? They need to know what they have to work on, don't they?'

Our vision can become blurred. Our worries and ideas and other people's expectations and opinions can get in the way of us seeing our kids clearly. We might fail to see that they are still perfectly them.

So, how do we regain that magical newborn feeling? How do we once again look at our kids with awe and gratitude? What can we do to make them feel accepted just as they are? That's what this challenge is all about! I have a very simple idea. It won't take long to put into action. It's not all the answer, but it's a beginning.

The Challenge

1. Tell your kids about the first time you met them. (This will work well for adopted children too.) You may have some photos and other things you can look at together.

2. Describe how you felt on that day.

3. Share how you still love them so very much and why.

I told my youngest daughter Gemma-Rose about the day she was born and how I'd felt. I said my heart overflowed with love. I didn't think I could ever love more than I did at that moment. But my love keeps growing and growing. How thankful I am to have Gemma-Rose in my life. I also told her how proud of her I am. I was specific in my praise. I had to look and think carefully about who my daughter is. I know Gemma-Rose is beautiful, but I wanted to go beyond the surface and talk about all the things that work together, making her a unique and special person. It was such a joyful conversation.

Even if you have no trouble accepting your kids just as they are, it never hurts to share what's in our hearts, does it? Perhaps we don't do that often enough. Maybe we should regularly repeat this challenge.

Could sharing our children's birth stories become part of our family's birthday traditions? Of course, I don't mean we should share a contraction by contraction account of our painful labours each year. We could leave out all that and talk about the more interesting details.

On my daughter Charlotte's birthday, I start her story with what happened the day before she was born. "Dad took us all on a strenuous walk," I say. "I plodded up a steep hill and reached the top just as everyone else was ready to come back down. They'd had time to explore and rest and were ready to go home." I remember turning around and rolling straight back down the hill. It must have been a cool day because I was wearing a coat. Drizzle was falling. The only good thing about the walk was finding a few forgotten lollies in my coat pocket.

That night, I woke up, knowing it was time for our baby to be born. "I groaned and told Dad I was too tired to go to the hospital," I say to Charlotte. "He'd taken me on that strenuous walk up the hill so I was exhausted." Of course, Andy ignored my complaints, pushed me out of bed, grabbed my hospital bag and drove me to the hospital. It wasn't long before Charlotte was in my arms. "When I saw you, I forgot about being tired," I smile. And then I describe how I'd felt as I gazed down at my third daughter. Surely there wasn't a more blessed mother than me?

We'd had a lot of trouble deciding on a name for our fifth child. "We liked Charlotte," I tell my daughter, "but your great-grandmother Charlotte got upset when my cousin gave her baby that name. She'd said, 'Why did you use that awful name?' But I knew you were a Charlotte when I saw you for the first time." And then I repeat the story of great-grandmother Charlotte's reaction to our baby's name. "She had a huge smile on her face. She said she felt honoured that we'd named you after her. I guess she changed her mind about disliking her name!"

Names are important, aren't they? While you're sharing your children's birth stories, why not tell them why you chose their names?

Related Reading

Perfectly Them: Radical Unschool Love

Unburying Our Love and Awe: Radical Unschool Love

28: Do Some Learning of Your Own

Years ago, I used to think education was only for kids. I'd been to school and completed my education. Now it was my kids' turn to work (and their turn to suffer). It was me against them. Some days getting them to learn anything was a real battle.

I've realised since those early days that learning is for everyone. It's not something just school-aged kids do. We're all going to continue learning throughout our lifetimes until the day we die.

Knowing that learning is life-long is exciting, isn't it? What have we yet to discover? What adventures are ahead of us? What passions and interests will we get involved with, and how will we use them? And if there's something we wish we'd learnt about when we were younger, well, it's not too late to learn it!

When we think of learning as something that only our kids do, we focus all our time and energy on them. We put aside our interests. We don't think about the things we'd like to know more about. We sacrifice what we enjoy for the sake of our children.

But our learning isn't a luxury. We don't have to feel guilty when we spend time doing the things we enjoy because we must be good examples for our kids. It's important that they see us learning, isn't it? They need to know that it's something everyone does. It's an essential part of life. It's just what we all do.

Also, excitement for learning is contagious. If we want our kids to love learning, we have to visibly love it too.

And if our children see us involved with our passions, there's a chance they'll be curious - "What are you doing, Mum? Can I have a go? Can I watch too?" - especially if we take an interest in what they enjoy as well.

Then there are times when having our own interests keeps us out of trouble. If we're busy gaining new skills and increasing our knowledge, we'll be less inclined to interfere with our kids' learning. We won't be hovering at their shoulders when they're involved deeply with something, wanting to direct things, and worrying about the value of what they're doing, because we feel at a loose end and not needed.

The Challenge

1. Think about these questions:

- What are you learning at the moment?

- Do you have any passions and interests?

- How are you learning?

- How do you learn best?

- Do learning opportunities arrive unexpectedly?

- Do you search for them?

- Do you learn something new every day?

- What if there was no such thing as school and even homeschool? Would your kids still learn?

- Do kids learn in the same way as adults?

2. Look for ways to incorporate some adult unschooling into your days.

At the moment, I'm interested in journalling, lofi music, body language, and having engaging conversations. I'm saying such things as "I found some *Star Wars* lofi music on YouTube," "Can I share some tips for telling humorous stories," and "I read an interesting book about why we should journal."

I'm also reading lots of crime novels set in remote parts of Australia.

Reading Crime Novels

I've been immersing myself in Australian crime fiction. I've read novels by Chris Hammer, Jane Harper, Patricia Wolf and S.R. White. I like the ones by Jane Harper the most, but they've all held my attention because of their settings. Detectives solve crimes in places with endless roads leading to outback towns where visitors who don't know how to survive in the heat stick out like beacons. Dust hangs in the air; the dirt is red; everything is dry.

We know what dry feels like even though we don't live in an outback town. We've lived through many years of drought and experienced starving fires racing through dry-as-a-bone bush towards our home.

During the last fire, when water-bombing helicopters flew over our house, hour after hour, and we breathed in thick smoke, day after day, I got fed up with the situation. I moaned to my family: "I bet the smoke is making me sick. It's inside me doing terrible things. I'm going to die. And when I do, you won't be able to bury me. The ground is so hard because of the drought. You'll have to wait until it rains. And that might take years."

My husband Andy laughed. "If we can't bury you, we'll cremate you instead."

"No, you won't! I don't want to be turned into smoke and ash!"

My daughter Imogen said, "If we put your body in the bush, the fire will do the job for us."

A bit of black humour to lighten our heavy dark smoky days.

A bushfire could be the setting for a crime novel, couldn't it? The murderer could throw the body into the flames. But he couldn't do that at the moment because there are no fires burning near us. Even though it's summer, it's unlikely a bushfire will arrive because it's raining. Again. Our roads are floating away because we've had record amounts of rain. But our home is safe. I sit inside in the dry, reading Australian crime novels.

Years ago, I found a list of the most popular Australian novels of the year and decided to work my way through it, allowing myself to give up on any books that didn't immediately grab my attention. I enjoyed. And I learnt. I saw our beautiful country in many different ways.

Approaching the same topic through the stories of authors with unique angles and styles is a wonderful way to gain knowledge, isn't it?

So is learning from experience: we know a lot about bushfires and drought because they're not just stories but part of our lives.

And now we're learning about rain. Three years ago, when there was so much smoke in the air that we could barely see the water-bombing helicopter in our park, we thought it would never rain again. But, of course, it did. We've had a couple of very wet years.

But one day, we'll be in drought again, watching the horizon: "Is that a fire approaching?" So that's why I'm not complaining about the rain outside. I'm happy, relaxing inside with my crime novels.

Related Reading

How to Get Kids to Do Their School Work: Curious Unschoolers

An Unexpected Opportunity: Radical Unschool Love

29: Record an Art Gallery Outing

I've read stories about teenagers who dropped out of school and into the world to obtain a real education. They spent their days not at home behind a desk but out and about, visiting places of interest such as museums and art galleries and seeing the world. And I've always thought, "What a wonderful way to get an education!"

Although we don't live close to any art galleries or museums, my daughter Gemma-Rose and I would occasionally hop on a few trains and travel to Sydney to visit the ones there.

And when we got home, our heads spinning with all the new things we'd experienced, I'd get out my homeschool records book to make loads of notes for the education department and our family journal.

When Gemma-Rose was 15, we went to the art gallery in Sydney to see the *Masters of Modern Art* exhibition. We strolled around the gallery, soaking in the impressionist masterpieces we'd only previously seen online as we listened to an audio guide. Now and then, we'd stop and exclaim over the colours and shapes in the paintings and share our excitement.

Before leaving the art gallery, I visited the shop and bought a guide containing images of all the beautiful paintings. I was buzzing: because of the book, I could enjoy the exhibition again and again. On the train home, I eagerly opened the book, but instead of feeling delighted, I was disappointed. I suddenly realised that looking at a reproduced picture isn't the same as standing in front of a painting and seeing it with our own eyes. I hadn't appreciated Picasso's art until I saw his work in the art gallery. The colours were stunning.

Although I was now aware of the limitations of images, I added many of them to my homeschool records book when we returned home. I wanted some reminders of our magnificent day at the art gallery and some notes for the education department so they'd know Gemma-Rose had received a fantastic art gallery education!

Perhaps you enjoy visiting art galleries as well. If so, you could do this challenge the next time you return from your outing.

The Challenge

Add the following notes to your record-keeping book:

1. A description of where you went and what you saw.

2. Photos of your children looking at the paintings.

3. A screenshot of a Google map showing the gallery location.

4. Digital receipts and information or scans of your paper tickets and the guide to the exhibition.

I added information about the *Masters of Modern Art* exhibition from the art gallery website. Part of the audio presentation that we listened to while we walked around the gallery was there.

5. Images of your favourite paintings from the exhibition.

I copied and pasted some from the Internet.

6. Some information about each painting.

7. Notes about anything you discussed with your children.

Gemma-Rose and I had a fabulous conversation while we were having our lunch. Amongst other things, we pondered this question: why is a plain black square considered art?

8. A cover image of any books you bought about the exhibition.

9. Find art-related resources to strew or add to a strewing notebook. Did your art gallery outing lead to any questions that you could research? Do you and your kids want to know more?

Here's what I added to our strewing notebook after we visited the gallery:

- Links to videos and articles about modern art and painters such as Matisse and Monet. (*The Art Story* website is an excellent source of information.)

- A cover image of the DVD, *The Monuments Men*, which we bought from the art gallery shop. It's a movie about a group of men whose mission was to retrieve masterpieces stolen by Hitler.

- A link to the Netflix movie, *Woman in Gold* about the retrieval of a stolen Klimt painting.

10. Reuse some older records notes if you revisit paintings or artists.

Gemma-Rose and I were already familiar with Klimt. I had some notes about this artist and his work in a previous term's notebook. Because we looked at the Klimt paintings and discussed them again, I duplicated the notes and added them to our current notebook.

One outing leads to lots and lots of learning experiences. After visiting the art gallery, Gemma-Rose and I read, looked and researched until our curiosity was satisfied. And I made many notes in our homeschool records book. Even though Gemma-Rose didn't fill in any worksheets or write an assignment about the art exhibition, we still had plenty of evidence of what she had learnt.

An Extra Challenge

You could record a trip to a museum in the same way.

And if you have few opportunities to visit galleries and museums in person, you could take a virtual trip online. Have a look at the *Google Arts and Culture* app or website.

30: Be Fit

Do you ever worry that your kids aren't getting enough exercise? They may spend a lot of time doing sedentary things such as playing computer games or reading books. Are you tempted to say, "Go outside and get some fresh air!"?

Years ago, I was always looking for ways to include some activity in my kids' days. Sometimes we'd go for a walk and do a scavenger hunt along the way. Before we left home, I'd write a list of things for us to look out for: a black cat, red car, picket fence, bike, or Banksia bush.

Or I'd organise obstacle courses in the park for my children to run around: "Run to the big tree, climb up the ladder, slide down the slippery dip, skip to the picnic table."

I didn't really need to organise these activities because my kids got enough physical activity by playing in the garden. Most days, they'd disappear out the back door and not return for hours. By the time evening arrived, my kids would be all out of energy (and very happy).

But what if we're not comfortable letting our kids play for hours each day? We might think they should be doing something more valuable (in our eyes) with their time. What if we sit them in front of the computer or encourage them to read or write or do other things which could be good but not very active? Will we end up discouraging our kids from racing around outside, playing imaginary games, chasing each other, riding their bikes, or climbing trees? Will we find ourselves saying, "Go outside and get some fresh air!"? Maybe we are part of the inactivity problem.

As kids grow, they could become less active. Some children might get to the point where they no longer want to play in the garden or go for walks. What if they don't want to exercise? After trying to force a teenager to leave her books and do something that raises the heartbeat, I learned that forcing kids to exercise is impossible. They might dig in their heels and refuse to cooperate if they don't want to do it. We'll end up frustrated and angry. So will they. It's much better if our kids decide for themselves that they want to be fit because this is a healthy and enjoyable thing to do.

So should we just hang around waiting for the day to arrive when our child might say, "I think I'll go for a run... join the gym... go swimming... take up a sport"? Or is there something we can do?

We could be a good example for our kids. We could make fitness a natural part of our family life, something important that we all do and enjoy.

We often want our children to do things we're not prepared to do ourselves, don't we? We want them to be fit and healthy, but we make excuses why we can't exercise. Sometimes those excuses are valid: we might not be in good health, or we're overtired because we're up late at night seeing to the needs of our babies and toddlers. But sometimes, we can do more than we realise.

The Challenge

1. Think about your exercise. Are you fit? Are you strong? Have you been neglecting your health? Should you be more active?

2. Can you find creative ways to include exercise in your day?

Instead of sitting in the car while a child has a piano lesson, could you go for a run or a walk? Perhaps you could use a sling or backpack to walk through the bush or around a park with a baby? Could you push a small child in a specially designed running stroller? Or could you arrange some time out for yourself to do a workout at home, swim a few laps, or visit the gym?

3. Find a fitness buddy (a family member or two?) to increase your motivation to exercise.

4. If you already exercise, do you need to recharge your enthusiasm with a new activity or piece of equipment?

How about searching for some YouTube workout videos, riding a bike or entering a fun run? You could buy some new shoes and a go-faster t-shirt!

If none of these suggestions is helpful, perhaps recognising that we need to be a good example for our children will be enough to motivate us to start moving. Like everything else, it all begins with us, doesn't it?

When I started running, my daughters asked if they could join me. Of course, they could! For the next few years, we all got up early each morning and ran together along the bush tracks close to home. We were The Team. We were fit and strong and had fun. It was a magical time of our lives.

Sometimes all our kids need to get moving is our example.

Related Reading

Should Unschooling Kids Live Balanced Lives?: Curious Unschoolers

Do Unschoolers Choose to Do Difficult Things?: Curious Unschoolers

Why We Don't Have to Push Kids to Work Hard: Curious Unschoolers

31: Speak with Trust

Do you trust your kids? I thought I trusted mine, but one day, I realised the words falling from my lips told a different story.

Many years ago, our oven broke, so we couldn't cook scones, muffins, cakes, and biscuits: all those treats we enjoy very much. I talked about this problem with my daughters while we ate lunch.

"We do have a microwave," I started to say. And then someone mentioned the doughnut maker, the toaster and the sandwich toaster. We wondered what treats we could cook using these bits of equipment.

"We'll do some research this afternoon," Imogen decided, "and then Charlotte and I will cook something for afternoon tea."

"Don't forget to do your music practices as well," I said. I looked at Charlotte's face and knew instantly that I'd said the wrong thing. It had dropped to the floor.

"Of course, we'll do our music practices," she replied.

"Don't we always?" added Imogen.

"I know you don't need reminding about such things," I said. So why did I say it? "When I was a child, I needed to be reminded. I wasn't self-motivated. Sometimes I forget you are different."

How often do we remind children to do things? I remember reminding Gemma-Rose to be good for me just before I went out for the day. She replied sadly, "Of course, I'll be good. Don't you trust me?"

Trust? Do we really trust our children to do what they need to do? Or do we think we'd better remind them 'just in case'?

I think about how I feel when someone reminds me I have to do something when I intend to do it anyway. It doesn't feel good. As an adult, I get very indignant. Should we give our children the same respect we give to adults?

But what if the piano practices don't get done? If a child isn't self-motivated to practise, they might not want to learn the piano that much after all.

I have heard stories about children learning the piano but always having to be nagged into practising. When they grow up, their poor mothers hope their kids will thank them for pushing them along and making them practise. So, is nagging a child to do something worth it? Will it pay off?

I don't like how nagging makes me feel. I feel worn out and drained when constantly pushing a child. I also feel at odds with them. Our relationship comes under threat.

I'd rather say, "You make the decision. If you want lessons, you need to practise. If you don't practise, maybe we should leave lessons until another time when you might feel more motivated." Because how necessary are piano or any outside lessons? Yes, they are a fine addition to an education. And I love to say, "All my daughters play the piano." But that's satisfying my need, not my children's. Anyway, if a child changes her mind, she can always learn later. It's never too late.

So Imogen is practising the piano because she wants to, and Charlotte is researching microwave cake recipes because she wants to. We want her to as well. We've been missing our regular blueberry muffins and savoury scones. All of us are looking forward to afternoon tea.

And I am trying to remember not to say the wrong thing because I do trust my children. I do respect them as people. Just sometimes, I fall back into unhelpful old habits.

The Challenge

1. Listen carefully when you're talking to your children.

What words are falling from your lips? Are you constantly reminding your kids to do things?

What are your last words before you part from your kids? Do you say, "Have a great time!" or "Be good!"?

If you have older kids, do you tell them to drive carefully, or do you say, "Enjoy your drive!"

Do your words reflect your confidence in your children? Do they reinforce your children's confidence in themselves?

Or maybe you feel you can't trust your children? Is that because you feel more comfortable keeping hold of control? Do you think this will keep your kids safe? Or perhaps you don't believe your children are worthy of your trust?

If you're reluctant to trust your child because it's uncomfortable for you, can you ponder the consequences of not trusting? Do negative words affect children's beliefs in themselves? Will it dent their confidence?

2. Once you've examined the situation, ponder the effect of your words.

Do you already speak with trust? Or would it be helpful to change your words when talking to your children?

3. And if you decide that you can't trust your children, can you find ways to help them gain the skills necessary to gain your trust?

Wouldn't it be good if we could relax knowing our kids don't need reminding to do what is right?

Related Reading

All About Trust: Radical Unschool Love

32: Strew Yourself

Do your kids ever say, "What are you doing, Mum?"? Or perhaps you're working on a project, and they ask, "How did you do that, Dad?"

Kids can be very interested in what we're doing, can't they? They often have lots of questions. And sometimes they want to have a go too.

Years ago, my girls were looking over my shoulder when I created my very first blog. They asked, "What are you doing, Mum?" I explained what a blog is and how I was going to publish my stories online where anyone could read them and my daughters said, "Can we have blogs too?"

Later, I changed the design of my blog, and my girls wanted to change their blog headers and backgrounds too. We all searched the Internet for free background images and told each other about our favourite sites.

I wrote post after post. I also announced I would do an A-Z blogging challenge, and my girls decided to do one too.

One day, wanting to tweak my design in a unique way, I explored the HTML section of my blog. Realising that changing the blog's code changes its appearance, my girls wanted to learn more about HTML and coding.

I commented on other people's blogs, and my daughters suddenly wanted to find blogs where they could leave comments too. We all found blogging communities where we could join in with interesting conversations and learn from each other.

When I decided to write my first novel, of course, everyone said, "Can we write novels too?" We all decided to take up the NaNoWriMo (National Novel Writing Month) challenge. And then we learnt about editing and publishing books together.

Whatever I did, my girls thought they could do it too. At first, they asked questions and then copied me. Later, they headed straight to Google to do their own research before experimenting with their blogs and writing. Soon their knowledge outstripped mine. It wasn't long before they were the experts, and I was saying, "I have a problem with my blog," "There's a plot hole in my story," "I don't know how to finish this post," and "Have you got any ideas for a story beginning with Q? Can you help me?"

After seeing me create a blog, my girls set out on a fabulous blogging and writing adventure. I quietly showed them a possibility, gave them ideas and did some strewing. I guess I strewed myself. You could strew yourself too!

The Challenge

1. Choose an activity you enjoy and would like to share with your kids.

2. Set yourself up where your kids can see you working.

3. Work quietly and wait to see if anyone notices what you're doing.

4. Answer any questions.

5. Let your kids have a go if they express interest.

6. Have fun!

It's good to share our interests, isn't it? There's something fabulous about talking the same language, understanding the process, working through problems together, feeling excited about the same things, and inspiring and challenging one another to learn more.

Of course, there are times when our kids are just not interested. They might walk past us, eyes glazed, their thoughts on something entirely different, not even noticing what we're doing. That's okay. Just keep doing whatever you're doing. Being involved with an interest of your own is a good example of learning for your kids. And who knows? Maybe one day, when the time is right, a child will sit beside you and say, "Hey, Mum, can I have a go?"

In the meantime, enjoy your passion!

33: Search for Delights

A couple of years ago, I discovered *The Book of Delights* written by poet Ross Gay:

The winner of the NBCC Award for Poetry offers up a spirited collection of short lyric essays, written daily over a tumultuous year, reminding us of the purpose and pleasure of praising, extolling, and celebrating ordinary wonders... The Book of Delights *is about our shared bonds, and the rewards that come from a life closely observed. These remarkable pieces serve as a powerful and necessary reminder that we can, and should, stake out a space in our lives for delight.*

I bought a copy of the book and began reading, and it wasn't long before I was eagerly searching for my own daily delights. Since I've been keeping my eyes open, amongst a million other things, I've noticed:

The golden evening sun reflecting off the topmost leaves of the gum trees outside our living room window.

White sulphur-crested cockatoos, resembling oversized flowers, swaying on the ends of bare winter branches.

The softness of our dog Quinn's velvet fur on the top of her head.

The smell of chocolate brownies wafting from the kitchen

The cold kiss of the early morning air on my face.

The excitement in a daughter's voice as she shares her ideas.

The thoughtfulness of sisters as they help each other.

The joy of a quiet hour reading a book.

Searching for delights helps when we're having a difficult time. Sprinkled between the challenges are gifts that remind us that God cares about us. We're loved, and there's hope. Despite the grey, there's still abundant beauty in our lives.

Delights encourage us to focus on the positives rather than the negatives of parenting and learning. Why worry our child hasn't yet conquered the art of spelling when she can still write delightful stories that make us smile? Look at the delight in our playing child's eyes! Does it really matter that our home is a mess?

If we look past the ordinary, we might discover the extraordinary.

The Challenge

1. Slow down.

2. Peer around.

3. Listen with attention.

4. Savour the flavours.

5. Inhale deeply.

6. Feel.

What will you discover?

Will someone envelop you in a hug of love?

Perhaps you'll appreciate the aroma of a good cup of coffee.

Will you take pleasure in your wriggling bare toes?

An exhilarating feeling may rush through your hard-working body.

Will you see a mushroom hiding under a tree, birds gossiping on a power line, a rainbow, or a dog riding on a motorcycle?

Perhaps you'll delight in a new idea.

Will you see beauty, truth and goodness?

Will your children remind you how uniquely wonderful they are?

Will you be glad you are you?

Related Reading

The Extraordinary Ordinary Things of Life: Radical Unschool Love

34: Waste Some Time

When I was a child, I always felt I should be doing something worthwhile. I couldn't just sit and dream, watch TV or read a book for hours on end. I had to be productive and not waste time. Often, I heard, "Isn't there something better you could be doing?"

As an adult, I've discovered that 'wasting time' is valuable. We learn a lot by doing such things as watching movies, playing video games, chatting over coffee, and reading comic books and magazines, don't we?

But what about those times when we're not even watching a movie? When we're not doing much at all, are we wasting time? Or are these times very important? We may need a quiet period after a busy one. When we're not doing much on the outside, could lots of processing be happening within us? Could ideas and thoughts be forming, dreams appearing, and connections developing? Or maybe there are times when our brains and bodies just need a rest.

Could learning not happen as uniformly as school suggests? Our brains might not be designed for ten weeks of full days of intense work before we get a break. Maybe learning ebbs and flows in a natural rhythm independent of the calendar as we absorb, process and rest.

What about our relationships? Could wasting time with our kids be precisely what they need? How about those times when we linger over lunch because we're enjoying the conversation, sit and listen to our kids who want to share their ideas, stories, and dreams, stop at the park, swing on the swings and giggle with delight together instead of rushing straight home? Do we need to slow down, soak in the moment and enjoy instead of trying to cram as much seemingly productive work into our days?

We won't always be able to sit and chat and listen to our children, giving them what they need so that they know without a doubt that they're uniquely valuable people who are very loved. Time with our kids is limited, isn't it? If we don't 'waste time' with our kids while we can, we won't be able to return and reclaim the opportunity later.

When our children have left home, we don't want to look back and wonder: did we do enough? Did we spend enough time with our kids, loving and enjoying and sharing the most important things in life?

The Challenge

1. Waste some time with your kids.

You could linger around the kitchen table sipping tea or milkshakes. You could stay up late munching popcorn and enjoying a movie together. How about snuggling in bed together on a cold day instead of rushing to get on with the day's work?

2. Allow your kids to 'waste' time in their own way:

They might want to chat, think, dream, rest, or play.

So, will you slow down and notice the delights surrounding you? Will you soak up the joy of spending time with your kids? Will you trust that what your kids want to do is what they need right now?

Will you waste some time today?

Related Reading

When Our Excitement for Learning Disapppears: Curious Unschoolers

35: View Learning a Different Way

One morning, just before sunrise, when Gemma-Rose was fifteen, we headed out into the cold for a run. My youngest daughter ran 10 km. I didn't.

Then feeling warm and tired, we walked home, chatting about our runs, the weather and what else we wanted to do that day.

We showered and had breakfast. We also did some chores. By the time we'd washed dishes, swept floors, and thrown a load of washing into the machine, it was 9:30 am.

"What shall we do next?" I asked.

"We could make some coffee while we wait for the washing machine to finish its cycle," suggested Gemma-Rose. "And when we've got the washing on the line, we could watch an episode of *The Portrait Artist of the Year* competition."

So that's what we did. Soon we were sitting on the sofa with the dogs, observing the different techniques of the various artists. We listened to people talking about colour theory and composition and how portraits can convey emotion and tell stories.

As the episode ended, we swapped opinions: "What did you think of the winning portrait? What did you like about it?"

And then Gemma-Rose said, "I'm going to practise the piano next."

She grabbed her music, and I grabbed my camera. Gemma-Rose's fingers began moving up and down the keyboard. Mine turned dials and pressed my camera's shutter as I captured some photos of my daughter at the piano.

Then Gemma-Rose asked, "Do you like this piece of music?" I said, "Yes, I don't think I've heard it before. What is it called?" Gemma-Rose told me the name of it, and I tried to guess the composer and failed. Gemma-Rose showed me the music and pointed out the grace notes, saying, "I'm not sure how to play those." She asked Charlotte to help her. Two sisters sat side by side as one shared her skills and knowledge with the other.

At the end of her practice, Gemma-Rose closed the piano lid, and I said, "I've found the first episode of *The Victorian Slum House* series online. Do you want to watch it?"

For the next hour, we went back in time, learning about the lives of the people who lived in the east end of London in the 1860s. As we watched, we swapped comments:

"How did the women make 1000 matchboxes each by hand every day? I couldn't do that."

"Can you believe that some people used to sleep upright leaning over a rope? Imagine not being able to afford a proper bed."

"They mended shoes with cardboard? That wouldn't have lasted for very long."

"Can you imagine working 16 hours each day and still being unable to eat properly or pay the rent?"

This morning, Gemma-Rose ran, helped me with the chores, watched videos, practised the piano, and chatted with me. And while doing all that, she learnt about history, creative arts, music, maths and personal development, health and exercise.

Using educational language, I could have translated everything Gemma-Rose did into notes for our homeschool records book. These notes might have satisfied an educational authority because my daughter learnt many things in the school syllabus. I could have ticked off a few boxes.

But I ignored the facts, figures, and school subjects and thought about other things instead. I decided to translate all that learning in a different way.

Running

Gemma-Rose set challenges, overcame obstacles, worked hard, felt encouraged and satisfied by her achievements, and increased her mental and physical strength.

Chores

Gemma-Rose worked hard and learnt about self-sacrifice and love.

Portrait Artist of the Year

Gemma-Rose witnessed people using their talents, following dreams, and experiencing the joy of creating. She thought about the best way to receive praise and the need to be humble and thankful for talents. Other people's work and ideas inspired her.

Piano practice

Gemma-Rose worked hard, persevering through the challenges of perfecting a musical piece. She experienced joy and cooperated with a sister as they listened to each other. She received help and encouragement, an excellent example for her to follow.

The Victorian Slum House

Gemma-Rose observed the value of gratitude, strength, family, love, resourcefulness, and compassion.

Do we place too much importance on the traditional education indicators when we wonder whether our kids are learning all they need to know? We're eager for them to learn lots of maths, history, science and other facts. But facts may fade, we might not be able to recall dates, and we might not remember all of a story's details. But there are other things that will remain with us forever.

Would we like our kids to learn about such things as love, compassion, joy, perseverance, and self-sacrifice? Are these more important than facts and figures? Will these change us into the people we are meant to be?

The Challenge

1. At the end of an unschooling day, think about what your kids learnt.

2. Note down all the English, history, maths, creative arts and other subjects they might have covered.

3. Now think about that learning from a different angle.

While your children were learning the traditional school subjects, were they also witnessing or experiencing love, compassion, humility, joy, cooperation, teamwork, self-sacrifice, forgiveness, the ability to listen and perseverance?

4. Record your children's learning in a different way than you would normally.

Are your kids learning the most important things in life? Are they becoming the people God created them to be?

36: Strew an Idea or Thought

When we think about strewing, we often imagine placing physical things where our kids will notice them. But that's not the only way to strew. It's also possible to sprinkle ideas and thoughts for children to consider and enjoy.

I'm always strewing ideas from books into my conversations with my family. When I read Austin Kleon's book, *Keep Going*, I shared the following words with my daughter Imogen:

Jacobs recommends that if you really want to explore ideas, you should consider hanging out with people who aren't so much like-minded as like-hearted. These are people who are "temperamentally disposed to openness and have habits of listening." People who are generous, kind, caring, and thoughtful. People who, when you say something, "think about it, rather than just simply react." People you feel good around.

Imogen and I talked about how like-minded is good. It feels safe and comfortable to gather with people who understand us. But is like-hearted better? If we're disposed to openness and listening, will we learn something?

I enjoyed our conversation immensely. Imogen and I exchanged thoughts, and we both learnt something new.

You could sprinkle some thoughts or ideas into a conversation too.

The Challenge

1. Share an idea that excites you with your child. Or share a thought you're pondering.

You could talk about something that you've read, seen or heard. Is there something in the news that's worth discussing? What books have you been reading? Do you have an opinion about a movie or a TV show?

You might drop your ideas and thoughts into a conversation while you're having dinner or washing the dishes. Or how about one-on-one times? Or while walking together? Car journeys could also be good times to talk with kids.

Strewing shouldn't be used to tell children what they should think or believe. Rather than trying to pass on your opinions, you could ask your kids: "What do you think?" And if they're willing to share, will you listen and accept what they say? Often our children have better ideas, thoughts or opinions than the ones we might be tempted to impress upon them. Even if we disagree with our kids, we could still have an interesting discussion if we're willing to listen rather than convince.

2. After you've strewed a thought or idea, think about the following questions and maybe jot down your answers in a notebook:

- What did you talk about?

- What did your children think?

- How did you feel about what they had to say?

- Did you hold back and listen rather than speak? Was that difficult?

- Where were you when you had your conversation?

- Did you both enjoy chatting with each other?

Related Reading

All About Strewing: Curious Unschoolers

Teenagers, Parents and Differing Opinions: Radical Unschool Love

37: Getting to Know Your Kids

When my daughter Charlotte was about five, we spent a few days at a camp with other homeschooling families.

On the second morning, I met a mother I didn't know. We introduced ourselves and said, "Which children are yours?"

All my kids except one were in sight, so I pointed them out. "I also have a daughter called Charlotte." I described what she looked like and then paused momentarily, wondering what to add. "She's quiet," I said firmly.

At that moment, Charlotte appeared, and I waved my hand towards her, saying, "There she is!"

The mother smiled and said, "I know Charlotte! I met her this morning when she joined my family for breakfast. She was very friendly and chatty. She's not quiet, you know."

Charlotte isn't quiet? Didn't I know my fifth child? Apparently, I didn't know her as well as I thought.

We may assume we know our kids because they've probably been part of our families since birth. We've watched them grow and develop. We've spent lots of time with them. How do we not know them? We might even think we know them better than they know themselves. And maybe that's the problem.

How often do parents say to children, "I know better than you"? We've lived longer than our kids, so we've had more life experience, which leads to the idea that we know best. But our kids aren't us. They have different opinions, passions, temperaments and needs from ours.

Of course, we can observe our kids and notice what makes them smile and cry and how they interact with others. But even then, we can get things wrong. Just like I did with Charlotte. Maybe we make assumptions based on our own experiences and what we hope is true and fail to see our kids as they actually are.

And then there's the part of our kids we will never be able to see: we can't look inside their heads, can we? What do our children think about? How do they feel? Do they have fears? What are their hopes and dreams, and what makes them happy? What do they keep to themselves?

Wouldn't it be helpful if we did have access to our children's minds? Or maybe it wouldn't make any difference if we could do that. Perhaps our own ideas would still blind us to the fact that each of our children is an extraordinary and unique being.

The Challenge

1. Think about the following questions:

Do you put aside your own ideas about who your children are so you can see them clearly?

Do you see your kids as you assume other people see them?

Do you listen carefully to your kids without talking over the top of them, especially when they're expressing opinions different from yours?

Do you value your kids' interests and the things that are important to them, recognising their passions are part of who they are?

Do you accept your kids' feelings?

2. Accept your kids the way they are.

Listen carefully to them. Show an interest in their interests, and get excited by the things that are important to them. Refuse to let other people influence how you see and treat your kids.

We'll know when we truly know our kids: a feeling of awe and wonder will envelop us when we're with them. Children are amazing, aren't they? They're caring and compassionate and have a huge capacity for work. They're curious and think deeply. If we listen to our children, we'll learn so much and see the world in a completely new way. They'll change our lives forever.

The other day, I suddenly realised that Charlotte is very sensitive. She feels things deeply. And this is okay. I should stop trying to toughen her up and accept her for how she is.

Yes, after many years of mothering, I'm still getting to know my kids. This shouldn't surprise me because how well do I know myself? I'm me, and I live inside my head all the time. But I'm still getting to know the person I am. At times, this can be disconcerting, but it's also exciting.

So who are your kids, and who are you?

Our Ideas or God's?

Simeon took the baby Jesus into his arms:

Now in Jerusalem there was a man named Simeon. He was an upright and devout man; he looked forward to Israel's comforting and the Holy Spirit rested on him. It had been revealed to him by the Holy Spirit that he would not see death until he had set eyes on the Christ of the Lord. Prompted by the Spirit he came to the Temple and when the parents brought in the child Jesus to do for him what the Law required, he took him into his arms and blessed God...

Holding a baby is an immense delight and privilege. We have a child that God has created in His image in our arms! We gaze upon the baby, unaware of what the future will hold for that child.

With our own children, no doubt, there will be times when sorrow will pierce our hearts, just like Mary's, but we'll also experience so much joy.

Babies look so helpless but wrapped up in their beautifully exquisite soft bodies is the potential to change the world in big ways and small, according to the mission God has given them. I never used to think about this. I was more concerned about growing children according to my ideas. It took me a while to realise that if we can put aside our preferences and allow our children to be who God created them, amazing things will happen.

That image of holding within our arms a child who has the potential to make a significant difference in the world is thought-provoking, isn't it?

Related Reading

When Teenagers Don't Know Who They Are: Radical Unschool Love

38: Help with the Chores

How do we encourage kids to help with the chores? Many people are searching for the magic answer to this question. Years ago, I also spent a lot of time trying to find the solution to the chores problem.

I designed rosters with jobs for each child for each day of the week. I wrote out lists of chores and let my children choose: first in, first choice. I tried a lucky dip system, disguised work as games and let my children experience the consequences of undone chores. By turn, I coaxed, threatened, pleaded, demanded, praised and complained. And yes, the chores got done, and we lived in a clean and tidy house, but my children only worked because I prodded them along. They never gladly offered their help.

I knew there must be a better way to handle chores, but for a long time, I was too busy and tired to search for it. With a baby crying in my arms and mess everywhere, I just wanted the jobs done now and quickly: "I've asked you for help. Please do it!"

Then one day, I realised something: I expected my kids to be willing and cheerful helpers, but I wasn't a good helper. I wanted my children to do something I didn't want to do. Of course, I didn't make it obvious that I was unwilling to help. I never said, "No, I won't help." What I did was agree to help but then fail to follow through. I stopped and thought about how I reacted when my children asked me for help.

"Can you help me with this please, Mum?" one of them would say.

I'd sigh and reply, "In a minute." Quite often, that minute turned into hours. Sometimes I forgot altogether. I didn't give my children the impression that I was eager to help them. Admittedly, there were times when it wasn't possible to help my children straight away. Babies and toddlers are rather time-consuming and unpredictable, so I couldn't always do things for my older kids when asked. But I got into a bad habit of never getting around to helping, even when nothing stopped me. Didn't I already do a lot for my children without helping them with all the unexpected little extras they wanted me to assist with?

I decided to try something new.

"Can you help me with this, please, Mum?" asked Charlotte.

I didn't say, "Maybe later," or "Can you ask someone else?" or "In a minute," as usual. "Of course I can," I replied, putting down my work immediately. I remembered to smile at the same time. It wasn't easy at first, but we can change old habits, and I discovered that my children really do appreciate my help.

My children followed my example, becoming willing and happy workers too. I'd found the magic answer to the often-asked question: how do we encourage kids to help with the chores.

It has to start with us.

The Challenge

1. Examine whether you're helpful or not. Be honest and put excuses aside. Do you always follow through when you promise to help your kids? Good intentions aren't enough.

2. When your kids next ask for help, say, "Yes! I love helping you!" Don't say, "In a minute," and then forget. You could say, "When I've finished doing this.. or that... I'll be glad to help. Give me ten minutes."

3. Help your kids with a smile on your face.

What if you're not in a position to help? Sometimes it's impossible to do what we'd like, but we can still have a helpful attitude. We can listen to our kids, giving them our time and attention even if we can't get up and physically assist them. Whenever I'm unwell or tired, my kids don't ask for my help. Instead, they want to help me. We all help each other when anyone is in need.

I've often thought about how little kids love helping with the chores, but then they lose interest as they grow. Why is that? We could pass on the attitude that chores are unpleasant and no one likes to do them. It's true they're often unexciting and can be hard work, but perhaps if we do them cheerfully, saying, "I love helping you!" or "It was a pleasure to do that for you!" our kids will view chores as something good. We can do them with love. Washing clothes and sweeping floors can result in joy!

Here's another thought: if we complain because our kids haven't done things to our standard, they might get discouraged and not want to help. This doesn't just happen with kids. Whenever my husband makes our bed, I'm tempted to redo the job. I prefer my way of bedmaking. But if I did that, Andy would stop trying to help me. I appreciate his help regardless of the result. We really do have to let go of our need to have things done our way, don't we?

Related Reading

The Right Question: Radical Unschool Love

Getting Kids to Help with the Chores: Radical Unschool Love

A Generous Attitude: Radical Unschool Love

The Radical Chore Roster: Radical Unschool Love

The Weekly Chores that Don't Always Get Done: Radical Unschool Love

Fairness: Radical Unschool Love

39: Go with the Flow

During difficult times, it's hard to keep up with the normal activities of life, isn't it? We feel overwhelmed by all we have to deal with. We might think we can't unschool because we don't have the energy or the time and inclination to strew, go on outings, and get involved with our kids' interests and passions. We could be tempted to structure our children's learning or even send them to school because we're worried we're not doing enough with them. But kids learn from everything in life. We might not be able to do the usual things with them, but they'll still learn. Difficult times are full of unique learning opportunities. They are very rich times indeed.

During our bushfire crises, I continually checked the status of the fires and listened to the weather reports and the Rural Fire Service's radio broadcasts. I prepared our home and garden and packed essential possessions so we'd be ready to evacuate our village if necessary. I talked to my kids about what we'd do if we got trapped in our house or car with a raging fire approaching. I spoke with neighbours and firefighters and swapped updated information. While smoke veiled our village, there was no time to think about ordinary things like homeschooling.

When the firefighters finally brought the fires under control, and we were able to relax, I thought about all the things we'd learnt: fire safety, fire fighting, first aid, back burning and hazard reduction, the regeneration of the burnt bush, home insurance, courage and selflessness, the compassion and love of concerned friends who sheltered us when we had to abandon our home, and a lot more. We hadn't needed to strew, read books, or go to interesting places. We'd experienced loads of learning just by staying home, watching the fires, and living our difficult but very rich lives.

We had another difficult time when my husband Andy was made redundant from a job he'd had for 25 years. Suddenly and unexpectedly, he was unemployed. Andy had nowhere to go and nothing to do each day for a while. He was also worried about not providing an income for our family.

But this period of our lives turned out to be good. We learnt the importance of pulling together as a family, cheerfully making sacrifices because of our money situation. Then when Andy was considering his options, we all agreed to continue living frugally while he went back to uni to get his Master's degree so he could set out on a new career: primary school teaching. Andy's uni experience reinforced our belief that it's always possible to learn something new and follow your dreams.

So, difficult times are full of learning. We just need to recognise this, let go of what we'd prefer to be doing, and be grateful that homeschooling is one thing we don't need to worry about when trying to cope with so much else.

The Challenge

1. Revisit a difficult time of your life.

You might have been sick, grieving, moving house, caring for someone unwell, pregnant, coping with a disaster such as a bushfire or a flood, caring for a newborn baby, or dealing with unemployment.

2. Think about the things that your kids learnt during this time.

Did they learn lots of facts or skills associated with the difficult situation? Did they also learn about the more important things in life, such as compassion and love?

3 Make a list of your kids' learning experiences.

4. You might like to label these experiences with a school subject and add them to your homeschool records book.

During a crisis, there's no need to keep up with everything you would normally do. Instead, you can go with the flow: let your kids learn from everything happening around them, trust they are learning what they need to know and draw close as a family. Trust your kids will be okay.

Related Reading

Learning from Life: Curious Unschoolers

Unschooling in a Crisis: Curious Unschoolers

An Unexpected Opportunity: Radical Unschool Love

40: Translate Shopping into Homeschool Records

Between lockdowns during the covid pandemic, I went shopping with three of my girls. We drove to a nearby city to the 'big shops', enjoyed browsing for books, clothes and makeup, and then had lunch before returning home. That evening, I was thinking about homeschool record-keeping. If necessary, could I turn our day into homeschool records notes? (We no longer have registered homeschoolers, but I thought this might be an interesting exercise.) So, here are a few things I came up with:

Maths

We added and subtracted as we paid for our shopping. Also, we used percentages because we bought a few things in the sale. We did all the maths in our heads and talked about how 40% is more difficult to work out than 50%. We used loyalty cards, and a few shop assistants asked if we wanted to sign up for new ones. We discussed the benefits of loyalty cards and compared different stores' loyalty programs. We'd allotted ourselves a shopping budget and discussed how we would spend our money.

English

We noticed which stores had QR codes at their entrances. We discussed whether QR codes are mandatory and decided they're only for sit-down customers in cafes. I remarked that 'mandatory' had become an everyday word because of covid. We then listed other words, such as quarantine, that covid has pushed to the top of the popularity list.

We talked about how language is changing and not always for the better. I told my girls about a news video I'd watched on YouTube about vocabulary. In some places, breastfeeding has been replaced by chestfeeding, a mother is now a birthing parent, a father is a co-parent, and a maternity ward is now a perinatal ward. This conversation led to a discussion about characters in animated movies. Are there too many blue-eyed, white-skinned characters? Do we always have to be politically correct?

Creative Arts/English

We browsed the bookshops, and after buying a few of Neil Gaiman's children's books, I shared a few things I'd learnt from Neil Gaiman's writing Masterclass. We talked about how some authors tell stories using only a few or no words. Instead, pictures tell the story. I bought a Shaun Tan picture book that has fantastic illustrations.

Creative Arts

I bought a drawing book by Johanna Basford: *How to Draw Inky Wonderlands*. We discussed the possibility of using an iPad and the Procreate app to try out the techniques in this book. This led to a conversation about drawing in general.

Maths/Geography

We used the shopping centre information map to navigate to particular shops using grid coordinates. If I were recording our trip as homeschool record notes, I might have included a photo of the info map plus a Google map showing our journey from home to the shopping centre.

Geography

We discussed the weather. The shopping centre is in a place that's always a few degrees warmer than where we live. It rained while we were travelling, and we talked about the changes in weather patterns over the last year or two. Not so long ago, we were in a scorching drought. But the weather turned cooler and wetter, which was a huge relief! We also talked about the seasons because autumn was approaching.

Personal Development

After we'd enjoyed our lunch, we returned to the cafe counter to thank the staff for the excellent food and coffee. We delighted the barista and also surprised him because not many customers take the time to thank the people who serve them. Working in the hospitality industry, my girls are very aware of this. Customers prefer to complain rather than compliment. My girls and I talked about the joy that results from doing little things like thanking people. We discussed phone etiquette and how rude it is for a customer to answer a phone while being served.

Religion/Personal Development

While in the car, we talked about Lent, which had just begun. We discussed our plans and chatted about sacrifices that look okay from the outside but are rooted in pride. Also, we mentioned there are times when we have to forgo a sacrifice because of a greater good.

Creative Arts/English/Personal Development

While driving home, we discussed the Disney movie *Mulan* and how the latest version differs from the animated one. What are the reasons for the changes? Is it better for a person to use her brain or her strength to win?

Maths

Close to home, we stopped to refill the car tank with petrol. We talked about the tank's capacity and the price of petrol per litre. Did our bill come to more than I expected because the car tank is bigger than I thought, or has the cost of fuel increased? I paid for the petrol, we travelled in Gemma-Rose's car, and Imogen drove. Charlotte provided stimulating conversation. We worked as a team!

Technology

While we were at the shops, the postman delivered a parcel to our house. It was my new phone. When we arrived home, Imogen set up the phone for me, which involved a lot of conversation about technology: backups, iCloud, face recognition, and updates.

Creative Arts

I took some photos with my phone using portrait mode and shared how I plan to use my phone. Would it be good for vlogging? Imogen suggested I make a vlog to test out the quality of the camera.

My girls and I chatted about many other things, but I hope I have shared enough to give you plenty of ideas for turning your own shopping trips into homeschool records notes.

The Challenge

1. Turn your next shopping into record-keeping notes!

How did you travel to the shops with your kids? Did you go by car, bus or train? Perhaps you went on foot? What did you see? What did you chat about while you were travelling? Did the weather affect your trip? Did you need to stop for fuel before setting out?

If you shopped online, did you discuss postage costs and delivery times? Did you order anything from overseas? How did you pay for your items? Did you talk about tracking?

2. At the end of your shopping day:

- Jot down all your conversations.

- Add a few photos.

- Take some screenshots of the websites where you shop.

- Scan your receipts.

- Find a map or two.

- Label everything with the appropriate school subjects.

- Add some tags.

You should have no trouble at all finding notes to fill up your homeschool record-keeping notebook after returning from the shops!

41: Add Joy to Your Days

Years ago, a mother told me she only arranges special outings with her kids as a reward. They can earn time with her by working hard on their school work, and then she will take them for ice cream, coffee or even lunch.

I felt sad that this family was homeschooling in a way that required rewards to encourage the kids to learn and that the parents rationed out the special times of their life. I wondered what the mother thought of me. Did she think I was spoiling my kids because I tried to turn as many moments as possible into ones that we'd remember with joy?

While my kids were growing up, we'd often go places with baskets stuffed full of picnic food, visit cafes for coffee or hot chocolates, and bake cakes for morning tea, lingering around the kitchen table long after our plates were empty, enjoying the conversation.

We celebrated everything from the first day of summer to the end of the music exam season. I expressed the love pouring from my heart by buying flowers and chocolates for my kids, writing love notes in cards, giving huge hugs and baking celebration cakes and saying, "I'm so proud of you!"

I tried to extract every drop of joy from those precious days of mothering as I could because I knew they wouldn't last forever.

Is it okay to turn as many moments as possible into extraordinary ones? Should we do that? Or could we end up spoiling our kids?

I think the joyful times of our lives - the smiles, the fun, the carefree days - draw us together with strong bonds of love. Those bonds give us the strength to face the difficult times when they arrive. Happy memories give us hope and keep us moving forward when we want to give up. They lead us back to joy.

And why settle for ordinary when we can have extraordinary!

The Challenge

1. Look for ways to add joy to your days!

Here are a few suggestions:

- Linger in bed with a child snuggled up beside you, savouring the warmth and softness of little-person skin instead of rushing to get on with your day.

- Talk with your children about their hopes for the day. Say, "Is there anything special I can do for you today?"

- Stop at the playground after visiting the shops instead of hurrying straight home, saying to yourself, "The work waiting at home isn't as important as spending time with my kids."

- Buy finger buns or another treat to enjoy at a picnic table next to the playground.

- Push your children on the swings. Have a go yourself, swinging higher and higher, feeling the breeze on your face.

- Use your prettiest mugs for morning or afternoon tea instead of the everyday ones.

- Find an opportunity to say thank you to your children.

- Help your child with a smile on your face, and then say, "It was a pleasure!"

- Give your children bunches of flowers so that they take delight in an unexpected gift.

- Make a snack and a drink for your child who's deeply involved with his latest interest. Arrange everything attractively on a tray and take it to him with a smile.

- Tell your kids how proud you are of them and explain why.

- Say, "Let's make some sandwiches and go on a picnic!" Then set off on an adventure.

- Suggest a walk to a local shop to buy ice cream.

- When your children say, "Can you please read one more chapter?" keep reading page after page of your read-aloud book until your throat feels scratchy and dry.

- Ignore the clock and sit up late watching a movie or chatting together.

- Hug a child tightly and say, "I love being your mother (father)!"

- Say yes instead of no, and see your kids' faces light up.

- Tell a silly joke or a funny story, and watch your children smile or giggle. Giggle yourself.

- At bedtime, say to your kids, "I enjoyed spending my day with you!"

- Chat about the delights of your day, and ask your kids to share theirs.

- Be thankful for your kids.

- Let your heart overflow with love.

2. Ignore all those misguided warnings about the dangers of spoiling kids, and refuse to ration out the special moments of life.

And remember: this precious time with your kids won't last forever. Extract as much joy as possible from today, tomorrow and every day while you can.

Related Reading

Why We Live a Life Full of Saturdays: Radical Unschool Love

Time to Unschool: Curious Unschoolers

42: Watch a Movie

Do you enjoy watching movies? When someone says, "Who wants to watch this movie with me?" do you rush to the sofa and settle next to your kids, eager to disappear into an onscreen world?

Could the time of day affect your feelings? Do you label evenings - when all the required work is done - as movie time and aren't comfortable tuning into a show earlier?

Or do you recognise all the fantastic learning that movies bring to our lives, so you're willing to turn on the TV or computer screen at any hour of the day?

Or could you be willing to acknowledge the value of movies but still be reluctant to let your kids watch them during the daytime because what will you write in your homeschool records books? 'Watched a movie'? That doesn't sound very impressive, does it?

But what if you could recognise the learning that your kids are experiencing as they watch? What if you could turn the movie into some acceptable educational language?

The Challenge

1. Choose a movie that your kids would like to watch. What kind of movie? Any movie. It doesn't have to be obviously 'educational'.

2. Make some popcorn and then sit back and enjoy!

3. When the movie is over, think about the following questions:

• What was the movie about?

• Did you like it? Why or why not?

• Did you learn any facts?

• What were the themes?

- What conversations did you have about the movie?

- Did the movie lead to any rabbit trails?

- Did you watch some behind-the-scenes or cast interview videos on YouTube?

- How was the movie filmed? Did you talk about the cast, settings, and costumes? What about the colour editing and the music?

- Are there other versions of the movie? Is it based on a book?

- Can the movie be labelled science, geography, history, English or creative arts?

Of course, we shouldn't make our kids answer this long list of questions about the movies they watch. It's not a movie study unit that they must complete. The questions are for ourselves. But, if your kids are like mine, you might discuss many of them without any prompting. As the movie credits roll across the screen, someone could say, "Well, what do you think?" And those words might be the start of a hugely enjoyable conversation about all aspects of the movie you've just seen.

4. Make some notes about the movie in your homeschool records book

5. Strew a few movie-related things

The point of this challenge isn't to spoil all the movies we watch by analysing them. No, it's to reassure ourselves that while our kids are enjoying themselves, they're also learning. Movies are an excellent way to learn.

Also, if we have to keep homeschool records, we should think about the learning contained within each movie so we can write lots of notes in our record-keeping book.

What if we watch a movie but can't see any value in it? What if the learning isn't apparent to us? The film might look like pure entertainment. Well, there's nothing wrong with pure entertainment, but we could consult an online study guide in case we're missing something. Just google the movie name and the words 'study guide', 'analysis' or something similar. Doing this might give you some ideas, opening your eyes to any unnoticed learning.

Years ago, I read a book by David Gilmour called *The Film Club: No School. No Work. Just Three Films a Week.*

Here's the book description:

Jesse didn't want to go to school anymore. After much deliberation, his father offers him an unconventional deal: he can drop out, sleep all day, not work, not pay rent, but on one condition - that he watches three films a week of his father's choosing.

What follows is an unusual journey as week by week, side by side, they watch the world's best (and occasionally worst) films - from True Romance to Chunking Express, A Hard Day's Night to Rosemary's Baby, and La Dolce Vita to Giant. The films get them talking: about girls, music, heartbreak, work, drugs, money, friendship - but they also open doors to a young man's interior life at a time when a parent is normally shut out. Gradually the father's initial worries are set aside as he watches his son morph from chaotic teenager to self-assured adult - who even starts to get up before noon. As the film club moves towards its poignant and inevitable conclusion, the young man makes a decision which surprises even his father...

The Film Club is a book that goes straight to the heart. Honest, unsparing, and emotive, it follows one man's attempt to chart a course for his beloved son's rocky passage into adulthood.

The father's and son's views about girls, music, heartbreak, work, drugs, money, and friendship differ from mine, so I'm not necessarily recommending the book, but I still found it interesting. It illustrates how we can connect with our kids while watching movies. Movies can lead to discussions about the essential things in life.

An Extra Challenge

Instead of watching a movie at home, why not go to the cinema with your kids? Go in the week when most people are at school or work. Buy popcorn and choc-top ice cream cones, flip down your seats, settle in and enjoy!

A while ago, Gemma-Rose and I saw *Emma* on the big screen.

When we arrived at the cinema, I bought our tickets, and Gemma-Rose searched for popcorn and choc-topped ice cream cones. Then we fought off the other seven Wednesday afternoon cinema-goers to get the best seats in the house. Nine people. Yes, there were loads of us wanting to see *Emma*.

The lights went down, and we settled back. The movie began, and we crunched and licked and watched. And then, unexpectedly, Mr Knightly discarded all his clothes, and there was a collective oooh! from all the older people in the audience. (Everyone except us.) Gemma-Rose and I grinned at each other.

The movie was good. It met our expectations. It was beautifully filmed, and the music was delightfully different. The timing was spot on: *Emma* was very funny. Best of all, none of our favourite moments from the book was missing.

At 4:30 pm, we stumbled back into the light and reluctantly rejoined real life.

As we drove home, Gemma-Rose and I talked about the movie:

"What did you think of Mr Knightly?"

'Mr Churchill wasn't that good-looking (in our opinion). Perhaps his appearance reflects his character."

"Weren't the costumes magnificent?"

"When Mr Knightley chastised Emma, did he use the exact words from the book?"

"I think they added that bit about Harriet's father."

"Emma's father was much more sprightly in this production than the others we've seen."

"The screens were very clever. They added to the humour."

"Did you notice that full stops followed the movie titles? Why was that? Someone's idea of style?"

Then Gemma-Rose asked, "What book would you like someone to make into a movie or mini-series? "That was the start of a conversation that led us from Jane Austen to Charles Dickens to Shakespeare to the Brontes and back to Jane Austen.

Movies can lead to delightful conversations in which we exchange thoughts and ideas and resolve to discover more. That's a fabulous way to learn, isn't it?

So, what's showing at your local cinema? Why not go online and take a look?

43: Have a Fantastic Art Conversation

I once wondered what would happen if I displayed a print of a famous painting on a wall at my children's eye level in a high-traffic area of our home. Would my kids walk past, see the picture, stop and look, and then want to talk about it?

I began with a painting by Vermeer, the Dutch artist, because I love his work. I hoped my girls would love it too. I used a high-resolution image file downloaded from the Wikimedia Commons website to print a copy of Vermeer's *Young Woman with a Water Pitcher* onto a sheet of A4 matte photographic paper. I framed the picture, hung it on the wall, added a label with the artist's and painting's names, and then waited.

"I like that picture."

"What nationality is Vermeer?"

"He's Dutch? That means he lived in Holland, doesn't it?"

"*The Winged Watchman* (a book we were currently reading) is also set in Holland."

I next printed a copy of Vermeer's *Young Woman with a Pearl Necklace*.

"You've changed the painting!"

"Look! Vermeer has painted another woman standing in the corner of a room. There's a window on the left-hand side in this picture too."

I found a book about Vermeer on our bookshelf. My girls were eager to find out more details about his paintings.

"Vermeer composed many of his paintings in the same way: a window to the left with sunlight pouring in, a table and a chair or two, and a woman in the corner."

While eating dinner, the younger girls wanted to share their knowledge with their older sisters.

"Can you see the yellow jacket that woman is wearing in *Young Woman with a Pearl Necklace*? It's made of yellow satin and edged with ermine. It's Vermeer's wife's jacket."

"Do you think Vermeer's wife minded her husband borrowing the jacket so his models could wear it?"

"Do you think she ever said, "Johannes, I want to wear my jacket on Sunday? Please make sure your model returns it by then."

Everyone giggled.

"The yellow jacket appears in many of Vermeer's paintings," I added.

"Do you think that jacket was one of his props? Photographers have props."

Then someone wanted to know what ermine is. Charlotte's guess was ferret. Imogen hurried off to get her tablet so she could do some instant research.

"Ermine is the pelt of the stoat, which belongs to the weasel family. The stoat is similar to a ferret."

We know all about ferrets. I let my son Callum have one as a pet some years ago. That was a big mistake.

"Were there bad weasels in *The Wind in the Willows* books?" I asked. The girls nodded. "Do we have those books?"

It seems we do. We have the original story by Kenneth Grahame. We also have the sequels written by William Horwood. Suddenly Sophie wanted to read them all.

I hung a painting on the wall, and my children noticed. They started talking and asking questions. We did some research and began discussing. One thing led to another. I think that was a very successful strewing operation. What do you think? Perhaps you'd like to do this too?

The Challenge

1. Find a painting that you like or interests you.

2. Locate a high-resolution file of it on the Internet.

3. Print out a copy of the image using photographic paper.

4. Place the picture in a simple frame.

5. Hang it on a wall where your kids won't fail to see it.

6. You could stick a note under the artwork with its name, the artist and the date it was painted.

7. Wait for someone to notice the picture and start a conversation!

8. After a couple of weeks or so, replace the painting.

You could choose another one from the same artist.

Or you could post a series of artworks on the same theme. How about still-life pictures? Or portraits? Or religious paintings?

Or you could mix up the paintings and try something different every few weeks!

An Extra Challenge

You could repeat this challenge using prints of drawings or photos of sculptures. Or how about displaying a photograph by a famous photographer?

44: Strew a Basket

On the floor next to my favourite seat in the living room is a basket overflowing with things I enjoy: a couple of novels, a journal and pen, a Bible, a DVD, my Kindle e-reader, my iPad, a set of Airpods and a bar of chocolate. Whenever I get a free moment, I dip into my basket, eager to read a few pages of an exciting story, listen to an inspiring podcast, watch a video on YouTube or write some notes about my latest delicious idea. My basket contains things I strew for myself. These are the resources that contribute to my learning.

As I said in the *Do Some Learning of Your Own* challenge, parents need to keep learning. We have talents that we should use, and we should follow our interests just like our kids. Also, we must be good examples of learning because learning isn't something that only kids do. It should excite us!

Even though we might be aware of the importance of adult learning, it often seems too difficult to do something for ourselves, especially if we're tired. Our kids and their needs keep us busy enough. But what if we have a basket full of interesting resources that we can't wait to dip into? Would that help?

The Challenge

1. Find a basket or a box (or a place to make a pile).

2. Fill your basket with things that interest you.

You could select a few books, a notebook, a Kindle or iPad, a colouring book, your knitting, crochet or embroidery, a list of things you could do online, or movies you want to watch.

3. Put your basket next to your favourite chair or where you can see it.

4. Use some of these exciting things when you have a free moment!

5. If you already have a strewing basket, you could sort through your items.

Are there some things you haven't used? Should you replace them with different things? Maybe you never got around to working on your drawing, sewing or crocheting. Do you want to take those things out of your basket and try something else? Did you finish reading your books? Or perhaps they didn't appeal to you? Do they need returning to a shelf? Should you look for a new novel or non-fiction book?

Extra Challenges

You could create a seasonal or liturgical year basket, such as an Advent basket. What would you include? An Advent retreat book, Bible, journal, music, things you're making for Christmas gifts, and a prayer list?

You could ask your kids to put together a strewing basket for you. They might enjoy strewing things that they think you'd be interested in. They could include some of their favourite things. Will you be tempted to try something new? I wonder if they'd add some snacks for you to enjoy!

Of course, strewing baskets aren't just for adults. You could put one together for your kids. Or how about giving them one each? Could you make a strewing basket just for books? Or your kids could choose their favourite books and pop them into a basket for a younger sibling.

You might have other strewing basket ideas!

There are only two strewing basket 'rules':

1. Only use what interests you.

2. And allow your kids to ignore things you might strew in their baskets.

You can always replace items. The world is full of interesting strewing possibilities!

45: Take Delight in Yourself

Are you glad you are you?

A few times, my answer to that question has been a definite no. I haven't liked who I am. I've wanted to run away from myself and my life. That's a sad state to be in, isn't it? I've needed to remind myself about the many delights of being me!

One morning, I took Quinn for a run through the bush during a break in the never-ending rain that had arrived to 'delight' us. The dog and I jumped over the muddy puddles on the main fire trail and sloshed through others too wide to avoid. When we got to our usual turnaround point at the bottom of the hill, I wasn't surprised when the rain started falling again. Huge soaking drops fell upon us, and soon my hair was plastered to my head. But that didn't worry me. I thought, "Who's going to see me? I'm the only person brave enough to go running in the rain. I have the bush to myself." I grinned and felt like a child splashing in puddles. I remembered my strong legs that can carry me up hills and my waterproof skin. I am fearfully and wonderfully made! I told myself I'm the kind of person who enjoys doing things that most other people avoid. I'm adventurous! And so I soaked up the delight of being me out in the rain.

A while ago, I got fed up with running. I was pounding along the tracks because I felt I should: exercise is good for me. I'd lost my joy.

So often, we lose our joy, don't we? We get overtired and overwhelmed and stop enjoying life. We forget who we are. Our days are crammed full of things that we have to do. Maybe we feel resigned; this is just how life must be. We're parents. We have to see to the needs of our families. There's no time to think of ourselves. But how can we look after others effectively if we neglect our own needs?

There is no doubt that being a parent involves sacrifice. We must be willing to keep giving and giving, putting our needs aside when things get tough. But if we look after ourselves when we have the opportunity, we may cope better on the difficult days and during the trying seasons of life. We'll have the strength to give ourselves to others when they need us most.

But what if life feels hard all the time? What if we feel it's impossible to think about ourselves? Could we have unrealistic expectations? Perhaps we're trying to be perfect parents, hoping to raise perfect kids. We may want to give our children our idea of the perfect education. Or we might think too much about other people's opinions, wanting to impress them.

When my first two children were small, I got into a lot of trouble trying to uphold my perfect-mother reputation. My friends used to say, "I don't know how Sue does it. Her kids are always immaculately dressed in ironed clothes. She cooks everything from scratch. And you should see her house: it's spotless and tidy!" Yes, when my kids were asleep, I'd scrub, sweep, tidy and iron instead of taking a much-needed rest. I had to be ready just in case someone knocked at my front door. What would they think if they visited and my house was a mess?

Looking back, I realise my kids didn't need ironed clothes, matching ribbons and French braided hair, and a perfect home. They needed a mother who had enough energy to spend time with them, playing, smiling, and taking delight in them. They needed to be allowed to explore and play with their toys and scatter them over the floor. They didn't need me following them around, tidying up as they dropped one thing and reached for another. They needed a mother who was less concerned about impressing other people and more concerned about them.

Often when we're overwhelmed, people offer help, and we say, "Thank you, but I can manage." Why are we reluctant to accept help? Why do we feel we have to do things by ourselves? Is it our duty to be self-sufficient? Is this just what parents are expected to do, and will people think we have failed if we can't go it alone?

Or should we let others into our lives, allowing them to share our days, and be part of our families? Should we be honest and vulnerable and admit that we need other people? Is this the right thing to do? Will helping one another result in love, joy and encouragement for all?

Our families and friends value us. They love the people we are. We hope they want to spend time with us, talking, exploring, pondering and doing things together. We want them to delight in us, but how can we expect them to do this if we don't take delight in ourselves?

Do we think we're delightful people? Perhaps when we look at ourselves, we see only our flaws. We might feel dissatisfied and disappointed with who we are. We often feel the same way about our kids.

Although we welcome our babies into our families with overwhelming joy and acceptance, somewhere along the track, we might start to criticise them. We could have particular ideas about who our children should be and find it hard to accept them as they are. We might not value their passions and interests that give them joy. We might also see faults in our kids and tell ourselves that it's our duty to correct them. We must make our children into the people we think they should be. We fail to realise that unconditional love and acceptance will dissolve any negatives - which might not really be negatives - and so we don't take delight in who our kids actually are.

Perhaps the first step to accepting our kids is to accept ourselves. Are we trying to live up to someone else's ideas? We may be okay exactly as we are. Could we already be delightfully us? Of course, we all have genuine flaws that need fixing, but love will have more chance of getting rid of our negative traits than despair, criticism, or disappointment. Unconditional love is miraculous. When I feel loved, I want to be worthy of that love and become the best person I can be.

If we want other people to love us, we must love ourselves. See ourselves as worthy of that love. Jesus told us to love others as we love ourselves. Sometimes it must seem we don't love other people very much at all.

So, what kind of people are we? Are we introverted, extroverted or somewhere in between? Do we need to socialise with others, gather with friends, and attend conferences and events? Or do we thrive on alone time and solo adventures? We could like meeting friends for lunch and having long one-on-one conversations about things that feel important.

Do we enjoy challenges and learning new things? Do we have dreams that have got buried under our everyday concerns?

Are we creative? Do we need to write, paint, garden or play music?

Do we like to escape into books or movies? Does secondhand shopping or walking around farmers' markets, searching for bargains, bring us delight? Are we tea people who savour quiet moments, trying out new blends? Do we love flowers and buy bouquets just for our enjoyment?

The Challenge

1. Think about why you love being you.

2. Ponder the things that bring you alive, making you who you are.

3. Regularly do whatever brings you delight. (Will you need to ask for help.)

If we delight in ourselves, we'll bring delight to others. Because delights travel, don't they?

Related Reading

Accepting Ourselves and Our Kids: Radical Unschool Love

Reinventing Ourselves: Radical Unschool Love

The Shaming Things People Say: Radical Unschool Love

46: Share an Interest

My children love sharing their interests with me. And I'm always thrilled when someone wants to know more about what I enjoy. It makes me feel special. It's as if someone is saying, "I want to know about the things that are important to you because you are important to me." We'd often rather get involved with our own things than share someone else's interests. But giving up our time is a gift we can give to those we love.

Being prepared to share an interest helps us see a different side of people. We might dismiss someone's interests as unimportant or even a waste of time. But trying them for ourselves might give us a different perspective. We won't really understand what attracts our kids to certain activities unless we get involved.

Sharing interests helps the bonds between our children and us grow stronger.

We may discover we want to follow our kids' interests too. But it doesn't matter if we don't. Receiving just a taste of what excites someone else is very valuable.

And if we're willing to share our kids' passions, they might be willing to share ours. They might show interest when we say, "I'm going to watch an art heist documentary. Would you like to join me?" Or "I'm going for a walk around the lake. How about coming with me?"

Here are some examples of sharing interests with my family:

When I tried playing the computer games my girls enjoyed, I realised how hard they were working. They'd developed concentration and critical thinking skills that I didn't have. My children loved explaining the games, suggesting tactics and being the experts. I enjoyed their excitement. We had fun together.

I once joined an exercise program that my daughter Sophie was doing. It was hard work, but I'm glad I did it because I could see Sophie loved sharing her fitness knowledge with me and appreciated having an exercise buddy.

The Challenge

1. If your kids ask you to join in with their activities, accept their invitations.

2. Ask your children if you can join in with their interests.

Take a turn. Ask them to explain what they're doing. Be interested!

3. Afterwards, think about these questions:

- Did you find this challenge difficult?

- Perhaps you had to force yourself to put aside your feelings about your children's interests?

- Or did you enjoy the experience? Did your children?

- Did you learn anything?

- Will you do it again?

You could end up playing a computer game, watching a gamer on YouTube, kicking a ball, riding a scooter, peering down a microscope, drawing or painting, playing the piano, making a bead necklace, taking fun photos, making a video, or having a tea party. There are a million things you might do!

Related Reading

Should We Push Our Kids?: Curious Unschoolers

Are Computer Games a Waste of Time?: Curious Unschoolers

47: Be Curious

Curiosity is at the heart of an unschooling life, isn't it, because it motivates us to learn? As we observe, question and search for answers, we find out about all kinds of things.

Kids are born curious, so they should have no problems learning all they need to know. But can curiosity disappear? Mine did. When I was a school student, no one valued my curiosity. I had questions, but nobody wanted to answer them if they weren't related to the school lesson plan. I had no time for wondering, pondering and dreaming because I had schoolwork to complete.

Eventually, I lost interest in learning. Sadly, when I finished my formal education after completing a Bachelor of Science degree, I threw all my notes and books in the garbage bin. I had done what was required: I'd got my qualification. And in the process, I'd lost my curiosity. On my last day of university, I breathed a sigh of relief and said, "No one can make me learn anything else." I no longer loved learning.

We don't want this to happen with our kids, do we? That's why we need to be careful. We mustn't stomp all over their curiosity.

But if kids are already looking at the world with glazed eyes instead of wonder and awe, there's some good news. Everyone can regain their curiosity. Unschooling allowed me to rediscover mine.

Have you noticed how curiosity is contagious? If we're constantly questioning and seeking answers, our children will likely be the same.

The Challenge

1. Slow down.

2. Look carefully at the world around you.

Maybe you'll notice a new road sign, read some words on the back of a cereal box that capture your attention, or hear something that makes you say, "I want to know more!"

3. Ask questions

4. Ponder possible answers.

5. Search for information.

Here are a few things I've been curious about:

After the 2019/2020 bushfire, I observed the regenerating plant life near our home. One day, I noticed some of the new leaves on the gum trees had been affected by a parasite or a disease. What could it be? Some trees had lost their burnt bark, and many others hadn't. Why was that?

We were curious when half the road leading out of our village was closed. Heavy machinery moved in. What problem were the workers going to fix?

During the covid crisis, we wondered how social distancing worked on trains. What if we got on a train and the carriage already contained the maximum number of allowed people? Would we have to get off at the next station?

Are the potato chips in the health aisle of the supermarket really better than the regular ones?

Did replacing single-use plastic bags with multiple-use ones turn out to be a good idea? Or are we now paying for thicker plastic bags we only use once because they need replacing when we forget to bring them each time we go shopping?

There are so many interesting things to ponder!

6. Don't keep your questions and answers to yourself. Share them with your kids.

You could say:

"Did you know...?"

"Can I tell you about...?"

"Wow, you won't believe what I just found out!"

"What do you think about this?"

"This is so interesting!"

Your kids may hear the excitement in your voice and want to know more.

7. We have no trouble satisfying homeschool registration requirements when we're curious people. At the end of each day, we should have many notes about all kinds of topics to add to our records books.

8. There's one more way to encourage our kids to be curious. We can answer their questions and listen when they want to share their discoveries with us!

Related Reading

Are You a Curious Unschooler: Curious Unschoolers

48: Make Fabulous Outings Notes

We all know that outings are packed full of learning experiences. While enjoying a picnic, strolling through the bush, or visiting a museum or art gallery, we're soaking up much information without realising it. We don't really need to think about it. Unless, of course, we have to keep homeschool records.

We can turn one outing into many notes, which might seem rather sad. Why spoil a good day out by viewing it as a source of homeschool records notes?

When my kids were younger, our Authorised Person (AP) from the education department expected to see lots of notes when she came to visit us at homeschool registration time. She wanted evidence that my kids were learning the required Key Learning Areas of the school syllabus. So I provided that evidence by making notes about the things my kids experienced in our unschooling life, including outings. If I hadn't taken every opportunity to turn unschooling into notes, I might have ended up with an empty records book. And if that had happened, would I have panicked and been tempted to make my kids learn particular things to ensure we had enough notes to show our AP? Anyway, record-keeping never affected the pleasure of a day out. I didn't let it!

So how do we turn an outing into homeschool records notes? Well, for some outings, it's obvious. We don't have any trouble making notes. But for others, we might get stuck once we've written, "We went to... and had a picnic." What else do we write? And even if we think of things to record, do we always make as many notes as possible? Do we always spot all the learning experiences that arrive naturally? Do we ask questions? Do we ponder? Do we want to find out more? Do we translate everything into the correct educational language?

One day, a few years ago, I suddenly suggested my girls and I leave our usual projects at home, forget about the housework, and go somewhere together and soak up the joy of the moment: "Let's have an adventure!"

Even though the object of our outing was pure enjoyment, I knew I'd have plenty of notes to add to our records book at the end of the day. This might have made me feel better if I'd been worried about having 'a day off' and not 'getting behind'!

"We could go to the nature reserve," I said. "Shall we take a picnic?"

Soon the girls were flying around the kitchen, assembling sandwiches and filling thermos flasks with coffee. And not long after that, we drove along the main road until we saw a sign pointing to the nature reserve. For more than 20 years, we'd driven right past that sign, never accepting its invitation. But that day, things were different.

We turned left onto a dirt road, swerved around a few potholes, bounced over a couple of cattle grids and found ourselves in the reserve. We parked our van in the empty car park, got out, and then looked around. There were picnic tables under some shady gum trees and a track leading down to the river. There was also an information board that we gathered around.

"It's a wetlands area," I said.

"It's a good place for bird watching."

"I wonder how many different species of bird live here."

We didn't head down the track right away. There was plenty of time. First, we sat around a picnic table and devoured coffee and finger buns while enjoying some good conversation.

When our hunger was satisfied, we set out along the trail that followed the river. We went around a bend and came upon a magnificent and unexpected sight: the river was tumbling over a weir creating waterfalls sparkling in the sunshine. Birds were hovering over the water, circling the sky, and perching on the rocks in the water. They were filling the air with a glorious song.

"Oh wow, look!" We all raised our cameras to our eyes and started clicking. We took photo after photo, even Gemma-Rose. She's not usually a photographer, but I'd offered her one of my cameras set on auto.

We continued to follow the course of the river.

"I can see a pelican!" It was sailing between the tree-studded islands that were floating in the water.

We took more photos. We captured everything: the birds, the river, the plants, each other and even the many information boards dotted around the reserve. Of course, we also read the boards, so we learnt about the wetland area birds and their adaptations to this environment.

We read about the reserve's ecology and how the rangers and volunteers are trying to eliminate all exotic species. We found a few signs saying *Do not eat the blackberries.* They'd been sprayed with poison. We also saw a sign that told us that another species not native to Australia, the fox, was being baited.

A few boards had information about the traditional owners of the land and their cultural associations with the area.

After we had explored the nature reserve from one end to the other, it was time for our picnic lunch. More photos, conversation, and soaking up the pleasure of being with each other on a beautiful summer's day.

When we arrived home, I opened my Evernote homeschool records book on my computer. It was time to catch up with the record-keeping while everything was fresh in my mind. I started writing, clipping and uploading photos. It was amazing how many notes I made about our morning's outing. I titled each note with a Key Learning Area, making it easy for our Authorised Person to see at a glance that my girls were learning the required school subjects.

Here are some of the things that I recorded in my notebook:

I added many photos of my girls, the river, birds, plants, the information boards and the warning signs.

I also uploaded some of the girls' photos after they'd edited them. (Creative Arts/Computer Technology.)

Sophie put some of her photos on Instagram with captions describing what we'd discovered. I mentioned this but could have added a screenshot or two if I'd thought of it! (English/Digital Media)

I added some Google maps of the area, including satellite and street views. (Geography)

I mentioned the information boards that told us about the birds and their adaptations to the environment. (Science)

I wrote down the main points of our conversations, including how the fox and blackberries are damaging the environment and upsetting the balance of the river and the surrounding ecosystem. (Science/Geography)

I clipped online articles with information similar to that in our conversations.

We had some questions, so we did some googling. I found some additional information about blackberries, foxes and other introduced species. Why are they considered pests? What exactly are they doing to the environment? And how can we control them? I clipped a few relevant articles into our notebook, saying, "Girls, you know how we were talking about introduced and exotic species this morning? Well, I've added some info about that to the notebook if you're interested." (Science/Geography)

One of the information boards mentioned a historic home we could see from the reserve. I did some googling to find out more. "Hey, girls, that house is called... "(History)

We wondered: the reserve was named after a person. Who was he? How old is the nature reserve? Who donated the land? What was its previous use? (History)

We searched for more information about the traditional landowners that the reserve is part of. (History/Geography)

We'd talked about the weir. Why do people put weirs across rivers? How do weirs affect the natural environment? We discovered the weir slows down the water flow in the river. Its presence formed the wetlands and the lagoon. (Geography/Science)

We went on a few rabbit trails:

I found a document online about the management of the nature reserve. We discovered that some time ago, during a drought, there was a proposal to remove the weir so the water could flow down to a local cement factory, but many people protested. (Geography/Science)

"Hey, girls, this is interesting! Kangaroos used to live in the reserve. A macropod fence kept them away from the river environment so they wouldn't disturb it." My daughters' ears pricked up, so I told them how the kangaroos used to be a local attraction. They'd come from different areas and were placed together in the reserve. They, therefore, had a different genetic makeup from the local kangaroo population. The kangaroos increased in number and became a pest. So it's not only non-native introduced species that can cause a problem. Sometimes native species upset the balance of nature as well.

One year, there was a lot of rain, and the river level rose and threatened to flood the nature reserve. The rangers decided to relocate the kangaroos to keep them safe. They moved them to another confined area. These kangaroos can never be released back into the wild. (Science/Geography/History)

Of course, we'd got some exercise while exploring the reserve. (PDHPE)

Sophie and Gemma-Rose wrote about our outing in emails and letters to friends. (English)

Summing up:

We had a picnic at a nature reserve. We took a walk and observed, talked and took photos. Mostly, we just slowed down and enjoyed the beautiful day and each other's company. I didn't lecture. I didn't ask questions that my kids had to answer. We just chatted and pondered naturally.

And then later:

- I uploaded the photos that we'd edited.

- I made notes of everything we talked about while at the reserve.

- I clipped articles that I found online that corresponded with our discussions.

- I googled the nature reserve and found out more about it. I clipped some of that information.

- I added a few Google maps of the area where we had our picnic.

- We googled the questions we were pondering and added the answers to our notebook.

- Being curious people, we ended up finding out more by following rabbit trails.

- I verbally strewed a few of the facts I'd discovered by saying such things as: "Hey, listen to this!" "This is so interesting!" "Did you know?" "I've put some articles into this week's notebook if you want to know more."

- I titled each note with the relevant Key Learning Area.

- I added a few tags such as 'genetics', 'geographical tools' and 'ecosystems' to relevant notes.

- I also quickly looked at the school syllabus to see if I could match up our outing to some of the outcomes, the ones we're supposed to achieve.

Why our outing wasn't a school excursion:

As I said, the focus of our outing was enjoyment. I knew we'd all learn a lot along the way. We always do. However, I didn't think of our picnic at the reserve as a homeschooling version of a school excursion. I didn't propose the outing to collect some notes for our records book.

In the same way, the extra information we googled when we returned was different from writing a report about our day out. It would be so easy to spoil a day by coming back and demanding our kids write a report, fill out a worksheet of questions, and do a presentation just like the kids do in school.

So why was our research different? My kids chose to do some googling, and they were free to listen to what I'd found out or not. Usually, when I have something to share, they are indeed interested. Maybe because I am. Curiosity is contagious. Anyway, finding out more extends the adventure!

The Challenge

1. Set out on an adventure with your kids!

2. Look. Listen. Walk. Explore!

Take photos. Eat a picnic. Ask questions. Ponder answers. Soak up the joy!

3. When you get home, do some research to find out more.

4. Add your photos, Google maps, notes about your conversations, relevant online articles, and other information about your outing to your homeschool records book. I bet you have many notes.

And you will have lots of memories. One day, you'll scroll through your homeschool records book and enjoy your day all over again!

49: Write Your Family Maths Story

Andy and I have 8 children, 3 boys and 5 girls. Our 1st 2 children were born 17 months apart, and it looks like there are 3 years between the births of the others. But this isn't true: appearances are deceiving. Thomas was born during the 3 years between Charlotte and Sophie. He died 28.25 hours after birth, and although his place in the family isn't obvious to outsiders, it is to us. We know he, and not Sophie, is our 6th child. She is our 7th.

There is a special relationship between our 5th daughter, Gemma-Rose, and Imogen, our 2nd. When Gemma-Rose was 11, Imogen was 20. When we add the digits of each of their ages, they make 2. When Gemma-Rose was 12 and Imogen was 21, these digits added up to 3. The following year, they were 4.

We love celebrating birthdays. There are only 4 months in the year when we don't get to eat birthday cake: March, June, August and October. In June, we eat wedding anniversary cake instead. 3 birthdays fall in summer, 3 in autumn, 1 in winter, and 3 in spring. If we add our ages together, what number would we get? It will be greater than our combined ages last year and less than next year's total.

I was born on a Sunday. So was Imogen. Sophie and Thomas were born during daylight hours, one am and one pm. The rest of our children were born after dark. Thomas died on a Wednesday at 3 pm, which is The Hour of Mercy.

Duncan is the tallest member of our family, and Gemma-Rose is the shortest. But she's only slightly behind her sisters, who are all just over 1.5 metres in height. (So am I.) That's about 5 feet. I won't reveal anyone's weight, but I can tell you some of us wear women's size 10 (AU) clothes, one wears women's size 8, and one buys size 6.

When Gemma-Rose was younger, she had hobbit feet, big for her age, but she grew into them. Her feet are now the same size as big sister Imogen's: size 6. The rest of the female members of our family have average-sized feet: size 7.

Except for Nora. Her feet are enormous. I almost forgot to tell you about Nora. She's one of the girls too. She's also a dog. When she was 18 months old - 1 ½ years - she weighed 23 kilos and was all muscle. I'm guessing she was a summer puppy, or maybe she was born at the end of spring. It's hard to tell. She was already 5 or 6 months old when we first met her in the animal shelter.

There are 10 chairs around our kitchen table. That's 1 for each member of our family, including Thomas. Of course, Thomas has never sat in his chair, but it's nice knowing he has a chair of his own like everyone else. Thomas' chair used to be the only empty one when we all sat down to dinner. Nowadays, there are 5 unoccupied places at our table because Felicity, Duncan, Callum and Sophie no longer live at home.

When someone sets the table for dinner on an ordinary night, we need 5 forks, 5 knives and 5 spoons. That's 5x3 or 15 pieces of cutlery. Add in the table mats, plates and glasses, and there are 5x6 or 30 things on the table. Usually, we need to serve dinner 5 ways. But if Duncan comes to dinner, we must divide the meal into 6ths (and multiply the cutlery by 6). If everyone came home for a visit and gathered for a family meal, we'd be dealing with multiples of 9 and 9ths.

I'm glad I have a family to share a meal with. Sharing is a blessing. For example, I discovered that 1/2 a cake tastes so much better than a whole cake when the cake is shared with someone you love.

Ordinal, cardinal, hours, days, weeks, months, seasons, weights, heights, ages, fractions, addition, subtraction, division, multiplication and a good splash of sharing. A family is all about maths.

Do young children need to spend a lot of time doing formal maths to learn the basics of this subject? Are all those attractive workbooks that try to teach kids such concepts as big and small, tall and short, and left and right really necessary? Could kids pick up all this maths information and much more just by living with their families? What do you think?

The Challenge

1. Write your family's unique maths story. Get your kids involved.

You could include the following:

- Ages of family members.

- The years, months, days of the week, and seasons everyone was born.

- The position of everyone within your family: oldest, middle, youngest.

- The number of years between children and whether they are older or younger than each other.

- If it's relevant, the date of your wedding. What day of the week and time of the day were you married? How many years have passed since your big day?

- Your heights, and your clothes and shoe sizes.

- Your pets, their size and their weights. How much food do they eat each day?

- How many people sit around your table for dinner each night? How many table mats, forks, knives, spoons, and glasses are needed? Do the numbers change depending on the day of the week? How many servings do you need to divide each meal into?

2. Add some details to your maths story to paint the picture of life in your family.

3. Add some appropriate photos.

4. Print your stories or copy them into a digital family journal.

5. Add them to your homeschool records book too.

6. Repeat this challenge regularly, maybe, once a year.

Maths stories can change over time. You might like to update the number of members belonging to your family, their heights, their clothes and shoe sizes, and the number of people sitting around your dinner table.

7. You could write more than one maths story for the same time period, focusing on different aspects of your family's life.

Your maths stories will contain many fabulous memories. They'll also remind you that family life is crammed full of maths!

An Extra Challenge

There are lots of family maths stories in a cemetery. Why not take a walk through the graves with your kids and read the headstones? Add and subtract the dates. Notice the decades and centuries. Work out the ages. Note the number of children. You'll discover all kinds of interesting things!

50: Find the Right Learning Angle

Years ago, a young friend - who homeschooled using a structured program - asked Sophie, "What's your favourite school subject?" My daughter said this question made her sad because if we have favourite subjects, we could also have ones that we hate: "I like science, but I can't stand history." Sophie said she thinks everything is potentially interesting.

Yes, if we're curious people, the whole world is a source of fascinating things to investigate. But this doesn't mean we will all enjoy learning about something the same way. Sometimes we need to find the right angle. Can we find a way into a subject that appeals to us? Can we approach it through the back door?

Years ago, I studied botany at university and got a Bachelor of Science degree despite not enjoying the course very much. Remembering all those cold weather excursions where I had no choice but to stand in the wind, a botanical identification guide fluttering in my numb hand while I sorted through millions of species of mosses, I'm tempted to say I hate plants. But that's not true. One of my passions is heading into the bush with my camera to take photos of the wildflowers. And I like looking at old drawings of plant specimens that explorers discovered on long-ago trips. I want to draw flowers too. I love the colours and shapes of succulents, particularly, and have made digital colour palettes from photos of these plants.

Doing experiments, going on field trips in miserable weather, and answering a million questions about plants during exams did not appeal to me. But I find plants exciting when I enter through my personal back door: via my camera, photos and drawings.

Why should we go to the trouble of finding the right angle to approach a topic? Surely, we don't need to know everything about the world? This is true, but could we find something that we might enjoy if we walk around a subject until we find the right entrance? Unexpected discoveries can be thrilling!

Also, if we're registered homeschoolers, we might be obliged to offer our kids the opportunity to learn the things in the official school syllabus. Some of these requirements might make our kids groan: "Why do we have to learn about that? It doesn't interest me at all." We could give our children a textbook and say, "I'm sorry, but this is what you're expected to know." We could try a few more unschooly options, such as suggesting a documentary or two, and then give up when our kids shake their heads. Or we could approach the topics more creatively. We could open them up to our kids in a personal and more appealing way.

When my youngest daughter Gemma-Rose was growing up, I had to find her the right angle into maths. She insisted maths was boring, but I wondered if that was because she thought maths was only about numbers on a worksheet or problems in a game that had to be solved before the clock ticked down. My mission was to discover Gemma-Rose's way into this subject. How could I approach it, beginning with the things that she loves?

Maybe you've also got children who groan when you mention particular topics. Would it be good to help them discover their own personal entrance into these things? They might end up enjoying them after all!

The Challenge

1. Watch out for a topic that holds no interest for you or your kids.

2. Walk around this topic, examining it from all angles. Can you connect it with something you or your kids are interested in?

I tried googling the words 'art history' together with 'maths' as I searched for a pathway from one of Gemma-Rose's passions into the dreaded subject of maths. My daughter ended up discovering that maths is very interesting and necessary when you want to sell your famous and highly valuable painting at auction. It doesn't matter if your work of art is a forgery as long as no one finds out!

174

51: Do Nothing Much at All

A mother once told me, "We had a day off today. The sun was shining, so I took my kids to the beach. They didn't do any learning, so what am I going to write in my homeschool records book?"

And I thought, "Oh my, I bet a lot of learning happened at the beach!"

I started making a mental list of all the possible things the mother and her children might have experienced and talked about during their day out together.

Here's what I came up with:

Did the children spread their bodies and float in the water? Did they sink when they moved into a vertical position, reducing the surface area in contact with the ocean? They might have watched waves poised high, ready to drop, potential energy soon to turn into kinetic as they rolled towards the beach. Perhaps the children anticipated the waves moving towards them, aware that they were full of energy that would soon transfer to their bodies, knocking them over.

When the children were tired, did they run back to their beach towels, noticing how difficult it was to move through the dry sand? Did the dry sand adhere to their wet bodies? Did it feel scratchy when they rubbed their towels over their skin? Did they feel like pieces of sandpaper?

Did the kids feel the heat of the sun on their skin? Perhaps the mother applied sunscreen to wriggling bodies while reminding them not to get burnt. Did she calculate when she'd have to reapply the sunscreen, looking at her watch, taking note of the time?

The children probably hopped quickly over the hot sand that had absorbed the sun's energy. Or did they wear insulating sandals to protect their feet? I wonder if the mother bought her children ice creams that dripped down their faces and arms as they melted in the heat.

Did the family wander across the beach, observing the fauna and flora: crabs, seagulls, seaweed, seahorses, barnacles, and trees? Did they stop at the rockpools and peer down?

Perhaps everyone exercised by playing volleyball or throwing a ball as well as swimming and running across the sand.

Did the children build sandcastles and collect shells and seaweed in a bucket? Did the mother take lots of photos? Perhaps a child had a camera too.

Did they smell the salt in the sea breeze.

While the family was at the beach doing nothing at all, perhaps they chatted about:

Conservation

Adaptations to the coastal environment

Habitat

Sharks, shark nets and safety

Safety in the ocean, surf rescue, what to do if you get into trouble

Sunscreen and skin protection, sun damage, light and ultraviolet rays, shade from umbrellas

Wave erosion

Wind erosion

Most importantly, did they have fun, make memories, and connect closely with the people they love best?

The Challenge

1. Next time you have a day doing nothing much at all, think carefully about everything your kids experienced.

2. Write down what they did, saw, heard, felt, tasted and smelt.

3. Make a few notes about your conversations.

4. Did your kids ask questions?

5. Did you provide answers?

6. Did you take photos or look at maps?

Did you enjoy your time together? Did you slow down and soak up the joy?

Did you do far more than nothing much at all?

52: Be Kind

Years ago, before we made our way back to unschooling, I often thought, "My kids won't do what I want if I don't yell, threaten or punish them." Life was stressful. I was often angry and upset. And unkind.

Yes, I was often unkind to my children, but I felt my unkindness was justified. It was my children's fault I acted without gentleness. If only they'd do what I told them. I believed it was my duty as a mother to push them, even when I didn't like what was happening to our relationship. I had to be tough and teach my children what was right.

But then, one day, I wondered if unkindness is ever justified. Is there ever an occasion when we can honestly say, "I had to be unkind? I had no choice."

I might not have considered this question if my unkind behaviour had been effective, but it wasn't. I eventually recognised my kids weren't the cause of my parenting problems. And things wouldn't be fixed if I hid my unkindness by smiling gently and refusing to get upset when my kids protested. I realised we just weren't living life as we were meant to. I should have listened to my kids, not to all those outside voices bombarding me daily.

So I made some changes. I stopped making my kids do all those things other people told me were important. The conflict dissolved away. And without me realising, we became unschoolers once more.

We often don't know what to do when raising and educating our kids. How can we encourage them to help with the chores? Should we make them learn particular things? Perhaps we should limit screen time. Should we force our kids to do what we think is important, even if they protest? We have so much to worry about as parents, don't we? So many decisions to make. What do we do?

We can start with kindness, incorporating the following principle into our lives:

Never do anything unkind.

If we have to be unkind to implement a homeschooling or parenting practice, we should reject it.

Kindness might already be at the heart of your family life, so is this challenge still relevant for you? Oh yes. We can never be too kind, can we? Plus, you might enjoy the challenge. When we're kind, we feel joyful. And joy is contagious!

The Challenge

1. If your family relationships are suffering, look at what's happening. List the sources of conflict. Are you pushing your kids to do unimportant things? Is your parenting based on other people's expectations? Can you let go of some things? If you're uncomfortable doing this, are there ways to gain your kids' cooperation without resorting to unkindness?

2. Look for opportunities to be kind. Give more than you are obliged. Go above and beyond.

Here are a few suggestions:

- When your children are engrossed in their passions and have forgotten to eat, prepare drinks and snacks and deliver them to their bedrooms, laptops, garden or wherever they're working. Why not use special mugs and arrange everything beautifully? The extra effort will delight your kids.

- Buy flowers for a child. You could add a few words of appreciation for what they do and who they are.

- Do a chore or two that your children are usually responsible for. You'll have to be quick, so you complete the task before your children arrive to start work!

- Recognise when your children are tired - they might get grumpy too - and take over their chores. Suggest they rest, soak in a bath, or watch a movie. Bring them a drink. Show them the same consideration you'd like when you run out of energy.

There are lots of other ways to be kind. If you're stuck for ideas, you could think of occasions when people have been kind to you.

What did they do? What did they say? How did they give you joy? You could do similar things for your kids.

Or you could just stay alert. Wear your kind eyes! When an opportunity arrives, you'll be ready to make a difference with kindness.

One last thing: our kids don't have to earn our kindness. We shouldn't wonder if they deserve our special attention. Our kindness is a gift, no strings attached.

If you take up this challenge, be prepared to feel warm and joyful!

Related Reading

Acquiring Bucketloads of Trust: Curious Unschoolers

53: Strew Something Old

Do you have a turntable or record player? Or maybe you've always wanted to buy one? Wouldn't a record player be a wonderful thing to strew? Imagine all the fun we could have hunting through charity shops and other secondhand stores for vinyl records. And think of the questions our kids might ask and the conversations we could enjoy. We could explore music from the past and look at all the album artwork. I bet a record player could lead us on some fantastic learning adventures!

Maybe you're too young to have bought a record player when they were popular, but I'm not. I remember saving my money, buying records and then listening to the same ones over and over again. I liked Police and Sting, Debbie Harry, the Eurythmics, UB40, and Fleetwood Mac.

The other day, while Gemma-Rose and I were in the shopping centre having coffee, we listened to the music playing in the background. The songs, which were from the 1980s, led to a fabulous conversation. We chatted about both old music and current music. I told Gemma-Rose about my life in the 80s. So many stories! I reckon sharing stories is a wonderful way to learn, don't you?

The Challenge

1. Find something old. Put it in a place where your children will discover it.

If you have a turntable, you could arrange a stack of records next to it. You could even choose one to play.

Or you could dig out:

- An audio cassette and a player

- A dial-with-your-finger phone

- An old camera, an album of photos, some negatives

- A typewriter and some paper

- A watch that needs winding each day

- A few medals or awards

- Newspaper clippings and scrapbooks

- A birth or wedding certificate

- An expired passport, bus pass, or student identification card

- A family Bible

- A wedding dress or suit (They might seem old to your kids even if you're not!)

- Some out-of-date fashions

- A piece of jewellery

- Old dolls, teddies, cars and other toys

- The contents of your treasure box

- A few movies from the past

    2. Talk about the old things you strew.

They might lead to interesting stories or send you on rabbit trails. They could result in some great conversations.

    3. Add details of your conversations, photos and any articles you googled and read to your homeschool records book.

An Extra Challenge

If you don't keep old things, you could strew a trip to a museum or visit a secondhand or antique shop.

When we last went to the National Museum of Australia in Canberra, one of my girls cried out, "Look! There's Jeannie Gunn's desk!"

We never expected to see the old scratched wooden desk Jeannie Gunn sat at while writing *We of the Never-Never*, a novel we'd just read together.

I also never expected to see a copy of the biology book I'd used in high school in the museum. Is it really that old? Perhaps I'm old too!

54: Collect Delicious Words

Do your kids like to cook? Perhaps they help you in the kitchen? While your children are cooking, do they use words that could be described as mathematical?

Do they talk about 'dividing' the dough into '6' pieces?

They may pour milk until the jug is 'full'.

They could line a 'square' cake tin with baking paper.

They might 'arrange' the 'round' cookies on a 'rectangular' tray.

Do they follow the recipe 'instructions' and ask, "What comes next?"

What mathematical words are your kids expected to know and understand? Maybe they're using some of them while they're cooking!

The Challenge

1. Listen carefully for mathematical vocabulary the next time your kids cook. You could also chat about what they're doing using mathematical words.

2. Make a *Mathematical Vocabulary* list of the words.

3. Add appropriate labels such as 'English' and 'maths'.

4. Include the list in your homeschool records notebook. (It's always good to add something other than 'used fractions while cooking' to our notes!)

Of course, you might find other cooking-associated notes to include in your notebook. Cooking is 'science' because many chemical reactions happen between selecting the ingredients and serving the final tasty product. You could add 'creative arts' if your kids make cakes and decorate them. And if you invite someone to enjoy your kids' cooking, you'll be socialising, and that's 'personal development'!

Extra Challenges

You could repeat this challenge for scientific vocabulary: food spoilage, allergy, vacuum packaging, acid, bacteria, aerate, liquid, boil, caramelise, carbohydrate, protein, fat and many other words.

You could also search for mathematical and scientific vocabulary in other activities such as sewing, running or gardening.

And you might like to collect words in novels that appeal to your ears. Gemma-Rose and I once found lots of unusual words in *Jane Eyre*.

Lost Words

This morning, a gorgeous word rolled off my tongue. I smiled and said it again. And again. What was the word? Unfortunately, I can't remember. It has disappeared. I lost it, which is very sad because it was so delicious.

I was talking about words with my daughter, Gemma-Rose, while we were travelling home from the vet with our dog, Nora. Do you remember," I said, "how you loved the word 'excruciatingly' when you were younger? And how about the words 'alabaster brow'? We found them in *Anne of Green Gables*."

Gemma-Rose smiled. "It couldn't have been Anne who had the alabaster brow. She was covered in freckles!"

"How about 'autumnal'? That's one of my favourite words. Now that it's autumn, I'm going to use it again and again!"

When we arrived home, Gemma-Rose said, "Could you please read more of *Jane Eyre*?" We settled on the sofa with the book and two mugs of coffee, and I began reading.

It wasn't long before I stumbled over a long word. Gemma-Rose grinned as she waited for me to sound it out. "Charlotte Bronte used a lot of complicated words!" I declared. "Some are hard to read out loud because they're unfamiliar." Yes, there are a lot of words in

Jane Eyre that we no longer use. I don't even know the meaning of some of them.

"Fillip? What's a fillip?" I highlighted the word in my Kindle ebook to see its meaning and said, "A fillip is a flick of a finger."

Next, we came to the word 'charivari': a cacophonous mock serenade. (Cacophonous is a wonderful word, isn't it?) And then I paused at the word 'extirpate' not because I don't know what it means, but because I like the sound of it. "I wish we could extirpate the rats," I said. A few days ago, a family of rats fled from the rain and took up residence in our roof space. We also saw one in the garage. Actually, I think that particular rat is dead. Every time we open the garage door, a terrible smell wafts out. I wish I could extirpate it.

"Do you know what I'm going to do?" I said to Gemma-Rose. "I'm going to highlight and save all the unfamiliar words in *Jane Eyre* that I like so I remember them. Then I'm going to use them. Drop them into my conversations."

"You'd better remember their meanings, Mum. What if you use them in the wrong way?"

"I don't suppose anyone will notice. Is it likely anyone has heard of words such as fillip?"

So I've begun a word list. A delicious word list. I'm not going to lose fillip or extirpate or charivari. I wish I hadn't lost this morning's fabulous word. I keep thinking about it. What could it have been? Do you think it will return?

I love delicious words. Do you?

Will these challenges super-tune your ears? Will you begin hearing and seeing all kinds of words you never noticed? Will you start using many delicious words as you bake, create, experiment, explore and read? Who knows? Your vocabulary, as well as your kids', may increase!

Related Reading

Wanting to Know How to Spell: Curious Unschoolers

55: Share Some Family Stories

I love telling stories, and my kids love listening to them. I share tales about my childhood and teenage days: what life was like, the places I lived, the experiences I had, the clothes I wore, and the lack of technology in days gone by.

I share photos or google items and events from my younger days, we look at Google maps of the homes I used to live in, and I talk about the painful times of growing up as well as the happy moments.

I talk about my travels, school and university days, and how Andy and I met and married. Then there's the story of how I became Catholic even though I'd declared that I'd never do that. I describe the grandparents they can't remember and how their paternal great-grandparents were deaf, and how this affected their lives, isolating them within their community.

I also like to tell stories of when my kids were younger. I tell them how I felt when I saw them for the first time, how my heart overflowed with love (and still does). I describe our days together: what we did, what they liked, and where we went. I talk about the brother they never knew.

Family stories bind us together. They tell us who we are. We have a shared history and belong together. Our stories also teach us a lot about such things as history, geography, science, and how the world changes quickly. We learn about our faith and relationships and how we're not alone when we struggle, grieve, get upset or feel pain.

There's a wealth of learning experiences wrapped up in our family stories, isn't there?

The Challenge

1. Tell some family stories!

Gather around the kitchen table at morning tea time, chat while eating dinner, or snuggle on the sofa with hot drinks. You could talk while walking or driving.

Will you tell a story to your whole family or share a special tale during your one-on-one times? Some stories are for everyone, and some are just for one person.

2. Jot down the main points of your conversations.

Did they lead to any related research? Did you look at any maps or photos? You could add your notes to your homeschool records book. Or how about starting a family journal to keep your stories safe forever?

3. Afterwards, think about these questions:

- Where were you when you were weaving your tales?

- What did you talk about?

- Did you go on any rabbit trails?

Most importantly, did you and your family enjoy sharing the stories of your lives?

An Extra Challenge

Have you ever noticed how kids learn to tell stories by listening to ours? Have your children got any stories of their own that they'd like to tell you?

Related Reading

The Curriculum of Life: Curious Unschoolers

My Angel Family children's novels are full of stories. Dad Angel loves to tell tales of his life. And his kids love to listen!

56: Reframe Concerns

Sometimes life runs along smoothly, and then, one day, out of the blue, we read, hear or see something that makes us doubt what we're doing. Our confidence starts seeping away. We wonder: are our kids really doing enough, are they learning the right things, and will too much freedom make them lazy? Are we irresponsible parents? Maybe we should make some changes to the way we're bringing up our kids. Should we stop unschooling?

Or are our concerns unjustified? We may be looking at things the wrong way.

Before changing anything, perhaps we can examine what's causing us to feel unsettled. We could ask the question: can I reframe my concern positively? I don't mean we should hide legitimate worries under smiles and a hopeful attitude. No, sometimes things are indeed wrong. But usually, when we think carefully about our concerns, we discover that we've got no real reason to worry. We might even realise there are advantages to sticking with unschooling.

Why do we feel anxious? Are we affected by outdated thinking? Or could we lack confidence? Perhaps we're looking for an excuse to revert to a more traditional homeschooling style because it feels safer to be with the crowd.

Years ago, I felt anxious about unschooling and a bit guilty too. All my structured homeschooling friends talked about the fabulous-sounding detailed programs that they'd spent weeks putting together. Everyone exerted lots of energy getting their kids to do this work.

In contrast, our days seemed easy. I didn't feel overwhelmed. My kids were happy. I wondered: surely we're not supposed to enjoy life as much as we do? Homeschooling is supposed to be hard work. Am I lazy because I don't make elaborate plans for my kids that cover all possibilities? Perhaps I'm side-stepping my duty by not insisting they do things that don't interest them. Isn't life all about doing things we don't want to do? Maybe I should push my kids even if I end up battling with them. It's just what I have to do.

Despite my unsettled feelings, we didn't return to a more structured homeschooling life because I couldn't face the accompanying conflict. Anyway, after thinking carefully about unschooling and reframing my concerns, I could see there was no reason for us to change how we lived. I didn't have to feel guilty. Unschooling wasn't the second-best choice. It was just what my kids needed.

Yes, we weren't unschooling because I was too lazy to write a program and insist my kids do it. I was still working hard but in different, more satisfying ways. Our days flowed smoothly, not because I'd given up but because I was listening to my kids and responding to their needs: we had no reason to battle. And my children were learning. Surely learning happens best when no one is fighting? Not insisting my child learn something she wasn't interested in or had no need of at that moment wasn't me being afraid to take control. I wasn't giving in to my child. I was refusing to waste time, hers and mine.

The Challenge

1. Make a list of any concerns and worries you have.

2. Try reframing your concerns.

Here are some examples:

Concern: I'm lazy because I haven't put together a plan for my children. I'm not preparing them for the future. They won't be able to get a job.

Reframe: I'm not writing a plan because I don't know what my children's needs will be ahead of time. I have no idea what the world will be like when they are ready to leave home and head off on their own. Before those days arrive, I'm sure some jobs will disappear, and others will replace them. New opportunities are constantly opening up. Instead of preparing my children for specific careers, I'm ensuring they love learning, so they can always learn all they need. If they lack a skill or some knowledge, it will never be too late for them to gain it. Learning continues past the school years.

Concern: I should make my children do difficult things because life is full of them.

Reframe: Kids don't need to practise doing difficult things. These will arrive in their own time. Already, my children choose to do difficult things when they see a reason for doing them.

Concern: My children are reluctant to do what I want.

Reframe: Our ideas aren't always the best ones. My children know what they need to do and what is important to them. Like all kids, they're wired to learn. They don't need to follow my plans. They're motivated to learn independently, so they don't need me to tell them what to do. Anyway, forcing children to learn things they aren't interested in is a waste of time. Real learning only happens when a child is engaged and wants to learn.

If you can't find a positive way to interpret what's happening, do you need to dive deeper into your understanding of unschooling? Or could there be a problem you should solve? Evaluating whether your children's needs are being met is an excellent way to distinguish between a genuine concern and something that just needs reframing.

After completing this challenge, you will hopefully feel less anxious about unschooling.

You'll also have some answers ready when people try to distract you with questions like "But what about the future?" and "Isn't it good to make your child do difficult things?" You'll smile as your responses roll off your tongue!

Related Reading

Making Children Learn What They Don't Want to Know: Curious Unschoolers

Preparing Our Kids for an Unknown Future: Can We Do It?: Curious Unschoolers

57: Write a Happy List

Have you ever noticed how certain things or activities make us feel happy? They give us energy and lift our moods. And this raises the spirits of everyone around us!

The Challenge

1. Make a list of the things that bring you joy.

2. Sprinkle your happy things into your days.

These things should be easy to do and not feel like a burden. You should want to do them!

Here's one of my happy lists:

- Go for a run.

- Have my toenails painted by my youngest daughter, Gemma-Rose. My 'happy toes' make me smile whenever I look at them.

- Wear lipstick even when I'm not going anywhere.

- Read a book.

- Pray and read the Bible.

- Use a pretty mug that feels good in my hands.

- Brew real coffee and drink special blend teas.

- Write something just for me.

Happy lists can change over time. That means we can do this challenge multiple times! Here's another list of the things that make me feel good:

- Get up early while my family is still asleep to drink tea, pray, write emails, see the sunrise.

- Read a paper book.

- Listen to a podcast while walking with our dogs through the beautiful Australian bush.

- Take photos with my DSLR camera.

- Learn something new: watch a Masterclass, Skillshare or YouTube video or google something I want to know more about.

- Run.

- Chat with my husband and kids, and drink some good coffee at the same time.

- Wear dangly earrings.

- Watch and listen to the birds in our garden and the bush.

- Play with words as I write.

- Snuggle under a blanket or with a dog on a cold winter's day.

- Watch an episode of *Masterchef* (or another show) with my family in the evening.

- Notice the small delights that surround me.

- Email a special friend at the end of each day.

So, what's on your happy list? What brings you joy?

An Extra Challenge

Maybe your kids would like to write a happy list too!

58: Embrace Gaming

What do we do if our kids want to play games on their devices for hours, and we're not happy about that?

We could limit their screen time by making rules about when, what, and where our children can play games.

But if we don't want to make rules- because they set us up for battles - we could try ignoring our worries, reminding ourselves of the benefits of gaming, and then let our kids get on with it (until our doubts overwhelm us once again).

Or we could embrace our kids' passion for gaming. Instead of just tolerating it, we could encourage it. Get excited and involved. Cheer our kids on. Share it. Learn more about it. Chat about it. Support this interest.

If we embraced gaming, what would happen? How would our encouragement make our kids feel? Would we learn anything? Would being involved and supportive help us understand our kids' attraction to games? Would our relationships be strengthened? Would we share in our kids' joy? Would a whole new world open up before us?

We could make rules and probably battle. Or we could let go and then possibly grab back control when our doubts once again take hold of us. Or we could try this third gaming option. What do you think? Is it worth giving it a go?

But what if gaming isn't our thing? What if we're reluctant to embrace it? It could be that we just haven't found the right kind of game to play. My girls tell me there's a vast variety, something to suit everyone, just like books.

Of course, we might try a few games and still not feel enthusiastic about this interest. We could say that it's impossible to get excited about something that isn't our passion and that we don't want to do ourselves. But is that actually true? Many parents spend a lot of time and energy encouraging and supporting their kids as they play the piano, sing or do other impressive things, which they themselves don't do. We don't need to have the same interests as our kids, do we? We can still get excited by their talent and want to encourage it because we are proud of them.

The question is: is it possible to be proud of a gamer? Perhaps embracing gaming is a good way to find out!

The Challenge

1. Embrace your kids' passion for gaming. Get excited and involved. Cheer them on. Say, "Can I have a go?"

2. Ask questions and listen carefully to the answers.

3. Find out more about your kids' favourite games. Say, "I learnt something interesting about gaming today. Would you like to hear about it?"

4. Ask your children for their game recommendations. Try a few games for yourself.

5. Watch some gamers online.

I sometimes do that. I never thought I'd be a person who enjoys watching YouTube gaming channels. Why watch someone else play a game? That used to sound boring, a waste of time. But now I love settling back and witnessing someone else's thinking. It's fascinating. And inspiring. It also convinces me that gamers have superior thinking skills, like chess players. We'd be proud if our kids played chess, wouldn't we? We can also be proud they're gamers.

6. Think about these questions:

- When you became your child's cheerleader, how did that make them feel?

- Do you feel closer to your kids because of your willingness to support their gaming passion?

- Do you better understand the attractions of gaming now you've experienced it for yourself?

- Did you learn anything interesting?

- Did you find a game you enjoy playing? Or are you still searching for the perfect one?

God and Gaming

Many people regard gaming as a time waster. Some Christians might also label it as a work of the devil. But there are some who embrace gaming and see value in it. They think that kids (and adults as well) are attracted to gaming because they're searching for a mission. Everyone has an inbuilt desire to live a purposeful life. We need to know that what we do has meaning. This desire attracts people to gaming, where they can set out on adventures to fight evil and protect the good. These virtual missions and desires may spill over into real life and increase virtues.

If you'd like to know more, you could check out the *God and Gaming* videos on *The Word on Fire Institute* YouTube channel. They might give you a whole new perspective on the value of gaming. Also, they'll reassure you that your kids will have many opportunities to make a career from their gaming passion. Did you know gaming is the biggest entertainment industry? And are you aware that there are many Christians involved in designing and developing big-name games? Gaming is what they believe God is calling them to do.

Related Reading

Why I Don't Restrict My Children's Time on the Computer: Curious Unschoolers

Are Computer Games a Waste of Time?: Curious Unschoolers

59: Make Time for Play

"Do you remember when we used to pretend the baby bath was a boat?" asks my daughter Imogen. "We used to climb into it and then try and move it over the ground using sticks." Her eyes glow. "That was the best game!"

It was just as well that I never needed that bath. I preferred washing the baby in the laundry sink.

"Do you remember when we built cubby houses under the pine trees?" asks sister Charlotte.

"Oh yes! Do you remember the day when Callum looked at our cubby house and said he could build a better one?"

"He pulled it apart and rebuilt it..."

"... and it ended up looking just like the one we made!"

The girls take satisfaction from the fact that their older brother failed to improve their cubby house design.

"Do you remember...?"

My children often talk about the fantastic games they played together when they were younger. As they remember, their faces light up, they smile, and my heart feels warm as I listen. My children have so many happy memories of playing. I know they regard their childhoods as special and extremely happy times. And because of that, I am glad I let them play for hours on end.

Unfortunately, I don't have any photos of the games my kids used to play when they were younger. I didn't get my camera out and snap pictures of their cubby houses, the baby bath boat or the tricycle that used to hurtle down the hill carrying more children than it was designed for. I wasn't a photographer in those days.

I now have a good camera, and I love documenting our lives by taking lots of photos. But my blog still lacks attractive pictures of my children involved in their play. That's because they no longer go outside and make mud pies. You won't find them swinging from the trees. There are no pine tree cubby houses, or even bed sheet ones, waiting for me to photograph. No, I still can't make my blog appealing with images of unschooling children absorbed in free play because my kids have grown up, and their play is no longer easy to capture with a camera.

My grown-up children play? Oh yes! I play too. Play is very important for everyone, regardless of age, isn't it? Play is the way we learn about ourselves and the world. It encourages us to use our imagination and dream big. Play is a safe way to test out those dreams.

We learn about relationships and other people when we have to play by the rules and be fair. And, hopefully, we conclude that we don't always have to win or have the leading role in games. Everyone is important.

Play leads to new ideas. It stimulates our imaginations, boosts our creativity, and improves our thinking skills. Play allows us to relax. It's fun. It makes us fun, too, because it encourages us not to take ourselves too seriously.

Perhaps the best thing about play is there are no expectations. We're doing something just for us.

Maybe when we play, we get an insight into our kids' need for play.

The Challenge

1. Set aside some regular time for playing.

2. Play!

What will you do? Will you do something alone or find a playmate or two?

Years ago, before Andy and I had children, I discovered some of my childhood board games packed in a box. The next time we invited friends to dinner, we showed them the games, and after a bit of reminiscing - "I had that game too!" - we opened a box, set up the board and began playing. Oh my, we had so much fun revisiting our childhoods!

These days, I like to play with the latest technology. In between the work of writing a book or a post, I play around with my blog. I try out different widgets, experimenting with them, wondering what I could do with them. Often, I don't end up using them, but that's okay. I'm only playing and having fun.

Not so long ago, I started playing video games. I had thought I'd never be a gamer because my first attempts to play a game ended in disaster. I tried playing *A Bug's Life* on my kids' PlayStation console but couldn't make my bug jump properly. I spent hours trying to complete just one level. Eventually, long after my family had gone to bed, I gave up, and with my head pounding, I vowed never to play a video game again.

Yes, that experience wasn't enjoyable. It wasn't my idea of play. Years later, after my girls insisted that there's a video game suitable for everyone and *A Bug's Life* isn't mine, I tried again. And they were right. I have discovered other games that are improving my concentration, critical thinking skills and imagination while providing me with a lot of fun. With play, enjoyment is the goal. Everything else is a bonus!

3. Play with your kids!

Kids need lots of time to play without adult supervision or even observation, but there are also times when they welcome our involvement.

I once joined in when my kids were playing a chasing game. "This will be fun," I thought. It wasn't. My long-legged son chased me across our backyard, getting nearer and nearer. I breathed faster and faster. And a feeling of panic washed over me: "He's going to catch me." He did. That wasn't much fun!

But I have enjoyed playing other games with my children, including board games. I must admit that when someone says, "Will you play this game with us, Mum?" I don't always want to join in, especially if I'm already doing something of my own. There are a couple of good reasons, though, why I try to say, "Yes, I'd love to play with you!"

Playing board games makes us slow down and concentrate on the present moment. To play properly, we have to push away all thoughts of our usual concerns. For a few minutes, all that matters is the game and the joy of playing it. And, of course, our children.

If we put aside our own occupations with smiles and glad hearts whenever our children invite us to play a game, what does this tell them? We'll be saying: "You are important. I love spending time with you."

4. Read Peter Gray's book *Free to Learn*.

Is it now time to play?

Related Reading

Is it Really Okay if Kids Play All Day?: Curious Unschoolers

Doing What Kids Ought to Do: Radical Unschool Love

60: Go on an Adventure

Years ago, when my oldest kids were young, we loved packing a picnic, grabbing the nappy bag and the baby, and then heading out the door in search of adventure.

Occasionally, we had fabulous spur-of-the-moment adventures. Once, after listening to our local news on the radio while eating breakfast, we found ourselves unexpectedly sitting on a beach watching breaching whales.

But sometimes we planned our adventures. Planning adventures? Is it okay to do that? Oh yes!

It's wonderful to head out the door on an adventure without warning, isn't it? What could be more exciting than hearing, "We're going on a picnic? Find the basket!" My kids never needed any preparation time. They'd have climbed into our van barefoot if I hadn't insisted they find their shoes. But I wasn't always ready to go adventuring. Other things claimed my attention. Days and even weeks would pass without us setting out in search of new experiences.

One day, I realised we needed to do a bit of planning. So I suggested that we turn every Wednesday into an adventure day. My kids liked this idea. So each week, we'd brainstorm ideas. Where would we go? What would we do? Did we need a picnic?

One day, many years ago, we decided to go to a nearby harbour for our Wednesday adventure. We'd driven past this place many times but not explored it on foot.

" Put on your exploring eyes," I instructed as my young, curious kids piled out of the car. "I bet we discover lots of interesting things."

And we did. Hidden in the rock pools along the shore were lots of fascinating creatures, including barnacles. We even saw a few sea horses washed up on the beach. In the distance, we saw a lighthouse. And then we spied the fish markets.

Soon we were trailing around a very fishy-smelling building. We watched apron-clad men and women with loud voices slapping fish onto scales before wrapping them in paper and handing them to the customers.

We pretended to be customers. What would we choose if we wanted to eat fish for dinner? Usually, we'd eat fish in batter, served with chips, of course. But that day, we were curious adventurers who wanted to buy something they'd never had before.

And then we became real customers, not pretend ones. When we returned home, one of my children was clutching a bag of mixed seafood, including baby octopus and squid.

Of course, the next step of our adventure was cooking our seafood. I don't remember how we did that. Did we add everything to a pan of boiling water? I do, however, remember my kids helping me. They all wanted to be involved. This meal was going to be special because we were going to eat adventure food.

I also remember how a couple of my kids didn't want to try the baby octopus. I didn't either, but I did! I discovered it was rubbery and hard to chew. (Perhaps we didn't cook it properly.) I didn't like it. Nobody did. But we'd tried something new. We can now say, "We've eaten octopus!"

After our day out at the harbour, we had a few questions. Where had the sea horses come from? What exactly are barnacles? What kind of fish is inside the batter when we buy fish and chips for dinner? Our adventure continued as we read books and discussed all kinds of fishy things.

The Challenge

1. Talk to your kids about what they'd like to do and where they want to go. The beach? The bush? The swimming pool? A ride on a train? A trip to a construction site? A museum? A market? A walk along the river?

2. Make a list of possible outings.

3. Add 'go on an adventure!' to your calendar!

4. Make sure you stick to the following rules for having fabulous adventures:

- Adventure with exploring eyes and curious minds.

- Talk about what you discover but don't interrogate or lecture.

- No worksheets allowed. If everyone's eyes are on a piece of paper, no one will see what's around them.

- Adventures are about being free to try new things and experiences – or not – without any pressure. Kids don't have to get involved with all parts of an adventure.

- No follow-up assignments are allowed. Required work kills curiosity and spoils an adventurous day.

- But it's okay to strew things later to extend the adventure as long as kids are free to accept or reject what we offer them.

- Focus on the enjoyment of the experience and being with each other. That's the best and most important part of an adventure.

An Extra Challenge

Why not watch out for opportunities to go on mini-adventures? Do you find yourself waiting while some of your kids have music lessons or other activities? Instead of watching the clock, wishing the classes would end, could you use that time to take some of your children to the park? How about you explore the fish section of your local supermarket? Could you set out on a walk down an unfamiliar street? On a cold winter's day, you could have a hot chocolate picnic in your steamed-up car and talk about the weather. Or how about visiting your local garden centre and coming home with a plant?

Adventures don't have to be complicated, expensive or take up a lot of time, and you don't have to travel a long way to find them. I bet there's an adventure waiting for you not far from your own garden gate!

61: Examine Your Words

A few years ago, I had an interesting discussion with my daughter Sophie after we'd been to a picnic with a few other families. Sophie had listened as a mother told everyone in earshot how lazy her daughter was. Her daughter was close by and heard the critical words.

Sophie was horrified that parents not only criticise their kids but that they do it in public. How would we feel if we overheard someone finding fault with us? What if they criticised us to our face?

Sophie observed two friends enjoying lunch together in a café where she worked. The women were halfway through eating their egg and bacon rolls when another woman approached their table and said, "You shouldn't eat that food. You're fat." She then pointed out that she had no problems with her weight. She was slim because she was careful about what she ate. The critical woman thought the two friends should follow her example.

Everyone in the cafe could hear the unkind words directed at the women. Their lunch together was spoiled: Sophie cleared away their unfinished meals. How must the friends have felt?

This incident makes me feel very sad. It's just not acceptable for an adult to criticise another adult, especially in such a direct, unkind, and public way, is it?

But what about children? We often hear parents pointing out their 'faults': "You're too shy... lazy... clumsy... thoughtless... noisy... stubborn... unkind... selfish. You should watch what you eat and exercise more. When will you ever learn to...?" They talk about their kids to other people. Their kids hear.

How do criticised children feel? Do they feel hurt? They know that they aren't loved and accepted just as they are. Could they be ashamed of who they are? Perhaps they feel like they're not good enough.

That could be the whole point of criticism. If we make others feel bad about themselves, they might do something about their 'faults'. But will they?

"Putting kids down makes them feel terrible," said Sophie. "It doesn't spur them on to do better. They just give up trying."

So what do kids need? They need to be accepted as they are. But what if they really do have faults? Surely we can't ignore our children's flaws? We can if we love. All the things we worry about might melt away under the influence of unconditional love.

"Sometimes parents complain about things that aren't faults at all," said Sophie. "These could be the things that make their children unique and special."

It's a pity parents don't see that.

The Challenge

1. Are there things about your kids that concern you? Write them down.

2. Do you express these concerns to other people in situations where your kids can hear them too?

3. Are these concerns legitimate?

Should you be worried about them? Or could your children's 'faults' actually be what makes them unique? Perhaps they just don't fit your idea of who your child should be? Can you turn the 'faults' around and see them more positively?

4. Make a list of all your children's positive attributes.

Do you use these words when talking about your kids? Or are you reluctant to do this? Sometimes it seems more acceptable to criticise our children rather than to say good things about them. We don't want to look like we're boasting about them, do we? But our kids need us to believe in them, be proud of them, and be openly in awe of who they are. Of course, our words must be sincere and mustn't be used to manipulate.

5. If you have genuine concerns about your children, can you find someone you trust to talk about them privately?

Often we don't realise the effect of our words, do we? So it's good to stop and listen to our kids, and let them tell us what they're hearing. We might assume we're saying things for their good, things they need to hear, unaware that what we're actually doing is tearing them down. It's sad to think we can hurt our kids unintentionally, isn't it?

Related Reading

Perfectly Them: Radical Unschool Love

An Active Approach to Radical Unschooling: Radical Unschool Love

62: Examine 'Trivial' Interests

Are your kids interested in things that you don't value? Do you ever say, "Where's the learning in that?" Surely your children aren't learning anything worthwhile while involved with their interests? Could they be wasting their time?

And what will you write in your homeschool records book if your kids aren't doing anything that's recognisably educational? A lack of impressive notes could be worrying.

But what if we walk carefully around a seemingly trivial topic, examining it from all angles? Will we actually find lots of learning that we never suspected was there?

Or perhaps if we listen to our kids while they're talking about their passions, we'll soon see all the ideas and facts wrapped up in them. I experienced this when my daughter Gemma-Rose wanted to tell me about some limited-edition eyeshadow collections she planned to buy online. After our fabulous conversation, I wrote this:

Are our kids learning anything while they're buying and applying makeup?

The other day, my daughter Gemma-Rose showed me some makeup packs she planned to order online. She wanted to buy a limited-edition collection of four eyeshadow palette sets: "I'm going to give one each to Imogen, Charlotte, and Sophie and keep one set for myself."

We talked about the colour palettes and which would suit each girl best. (Creative Arts)

Gemma-Rose showed me a bundle pack of makeup. Was it cheaper than buying each item individually? After calculating the cost of each eyeshadow palette in the limited-edition collection, she figured out that the bundle was exceptional value. She'd also compared that price to similar items available in our local pharmacy. (Maths)

Gemma-Rose told me that the makeup doesn't contain carmine because the products are vegan. Did you know that carmine is a red pigment derived from beetles? The beetles live on cacti and are native to Latin America. There are carmine farms!

I did a quick bit of googling and discovered that carmine is also known as cochineal. I told Gemma-Rose that red food colouring is sometimes known as cochineal. Together, we googled and found out that Skittles contain this pigment, and Jelly Babies are glazed with an extract from a different beetle. So these sweets or lollies aren't suitable for vegans. (Science, Geography, Personal Development)

Gemma-Rose told me that her makeup isn't tested on animals, so it's vegan in more than one way. She said that the makeup sold by this company can't be exported to China because the Chinese government requires all makeup to be tested on animals before being used on people. (Personal Development, Geography, Science.)

Our conversation then turned to other dyes, such as the purple dye extracted from sea shells, which the Romans greatly valued. We talked about how the emperor wore purple and why purple is considered the colour of royalty. We also shared stories of all the dangerous makeup products used throughout history. Oh my, it's horrifying to think of the health risks women of the past unknowingly took while making themselves look beautiful! (Science, Geography, History.)

Gemma-Rose is planning to give the makeup she orders to her sisters as a gift. This generous act could be labelled as Personal Development.

Using the Internet to make her purchases involved Technology.

I bet I could find lots of information about makeup and dyes to share with my daughter, but Gemma-Rose seems to be doing an excellent job of extending her knowledge herself. She's been using the Internet to google information. (Technology)

An interest in something like makeup might sound trivial and not very important, but when we dig a bit deeper, we can see it involves a lot of learning experiences.

Your kids might not have a passion for makeup. However, they could love gaming, skateboarding, hairstyling, watching superhero movies, playing with Disney princesses, reading comics or shopping for clothes. Whatever their interests, I bet there are loads of learning experiences hidden inside your children's favourite pastimes.

The Challenge

1. Immerse yourself in your kids' worlds.

Talk to your children about their passions. Find out why they enjoy what they do. What is it that attracts them to their interests? What are they learning? Of course, you mustn't interrogate your kids! Just take an interest in their interests. Be genuine, ask questions, chat and listen.

2. Do some research to find out more about these interests.

3. Make some notes about the different learning experiences associated with your children's passions.

If children are interested in fashion, they could be learning about:

Fashion shows - music, fashion design, performance, filming. (Technology, Creative Arts)

Fashion models - fame, style, marketing, body image, diet-related issues. (Maths, Personal Development and Health, Creative Arts)

Fast fashion - do kids know what happens to cast-off clothing? Recycling, charity shops, reducing waste. (Science, Geography)

Fabrics - natural and artificial fibres. Do children know why wool is warmer than synthetic yarns? (Science)

Fashion design - drawing, colour, designing for all body types and not just for super slim models. (Creative Arts, Personal Health and Development) Pattern making - lines and angles, sizes and measurements. (Maths)

Sewing clothes and costumes. (Creative Arts) Do kids know how people constructed clothes during different periods of history?

Do they know about mills and factories, and sewing machines and how they work? (History, Science)

Do kids know where their clothes were made? What about ethical issues? (Geography, Personal Development)

Costumes - movies and books. (Creative Arts, English)

Fashion image - photography, videography, and social media sites such as Instagram and branding. What do our clothes say about us? (Personal Development, Creative Arts, Technology)

Fashion history - Have kids noticed the fashions in period dramas and other historical movies? (History)

Cultural fashion (Geography, Religion)

Here are some other quick examples that you could expand:

Gaming - game design, teamwork, fine motor skills, conversation skills, public speaking, storytelling, reading, art, perseverance, strategy, decision making, missions and virtues

Superheroes - myths and legends, fitness, storytelling, videography, film analysis, science associated with superpowers, good versus evil, comics, reading

4. Turn all the learning you discover into educational language and add some notes to your homeschool record book.

5. If you discover any exciting resources while researching your children's passions, you could strew them to extend the learning.

Of course, you'll need to be careful not to push. It's so easy for us to give our kids the idea that we're not satisfied with what they're doing: "Okay, you can spend your time gaming... as long as you investigate these resources I've found and go down these rabbit trails and do some real learning..." Perhaps we need to offer our resources with detachment. If our kids reject them, that's okay. Anyway, kids are good at researching and following rabbit trails by themselves. Wanting to know more is part of having a passion!

Related Reading

When a Child Has Only One Interest: Curious Unschoolers

63: Find Common Ground

A few years ago, I received the following comment on my blog:

"Why would you post a picture of your dead baby online? That's just horrible."

The words tore at my mother's heart. That dead person was my son.

I deleted that comment. I didn't even think about it. I just wanted it to disappear as quickly as possible.

I only later wondered if I had done the right thing. I had responded emotionally, concerned only about my feelings. But what about the commenter? Why did she say those hurtful words? Was she just a troll not worth worrying about? Or could she have been afraid of death?

If I could go back, this is what I would have replied

I'm sorry the photo of my son disturbed you. I posted it because I don't have any pictures of him when he was alive except for the ones we took when he was hooked up to multiple wires and tubes.

It's rather confronting to see a dead body, isn't it, especially if you're not expecting to see one? Dead bodies used to make me feel uncomfortable too. But after my son died, I realised I had nothing to fear. He was still beautiful, even though he was no longer alive.

With carefully chosen words, we might connect with people who disagree with us. We can open the way for a possible conversation. When we react emotionally, we lose the chance to change people's opinions or hearts.

Although you'll probably never have to worry about photos of dead bodies, you might have to defend your decision to unschool. Yes, unschooling has its critics. And many of them have loud voices.

We could choose to ignore these people, and maybe that's sometimes the right thing to do. We don't want to waste time trying to persuade a troll that he's wrong and we're right. But perhaps it's at least worth trying to open up unschooling conversations with our family and friends. Wouldn't it be wonderful if they could see things through our eyes and support us?

So what do we do?

Instead of reacting to a critical comment, can we find something we can agree with? Can we build a bridge, making a discussion possible?

The Challenge

1. The next time someone criticises your choices decide if it's worth building a bridge.

2. Think about the critical comment. Is there something within it that you can agree with?

3. Try to start a conversation by beginning with your bridge.

Here are a few examples of opening statements that I've used:

Yes, unschooling does seem neglectful, doesn't it? I used to think it was, too, until I read...

Yes, it's not acceptable for children to be undisciplined and selfish. Maybe the family you're describing aren't actually unschoolers. Have you heard about unparenting?

Yes, it sounds like kids won't learn if we don't force them, doesn't it? But they do. Would you like to hear what my kids chose to do this week?

Does this challenge sound too hard? If it's not easy finding the right words quickly, you could practice during online conversations where you can stop and think between reading a comment and writing a response. Take your time. Move words around. Don't hit 'publish' until you're completely happy with what you've said.

Sometimes our efforts to build bridges are rewarded. Sometimes they're not. But at least we've tried.

Related Reading

Responding to Unschooling Critics: Radical Unschool Love

64: Create Family Traditions

Traditions are important, aren't they? They bind our families together, they bring a sense of comfort and belonging, and they might deepen our faith. They certainly create memories. And they result in joy.

Some time ago, we visited my parents for a Christmas get-together, and while exchanging gifts, my mother told a story about her most memorable childhood Christmas. When she was four, her sister was two, and her brother was six, the three children shared a double bed on Christmas Eve. In the middle of the night, they woke up to discover that Santa had left pillowcases full of presents. Amongst the gifts were a dump truck, a bag of sand, and a box of toffees. The excited children played for a while and then fell asleep amongst the Christmas mess. When my grandmother woke in the morning, she discovered three happy and sticky children in a bed full of sand and toffees. The way my mother told the story, I could see that these were magical memories of her childhood.

My mother told us another story: she and her siblings wrote to Santa every year before Christmas, scribbling down what they hoped he'd bring them. When the children had finished their letters, my grandmother took them into the living room to the massive fireplace that could easily accommodate a fat, jolly person. They placed the hopeful notes in the fireplace, and then my grandmother said everyone had to go into the hall so that Santa could come down the chimney to collect them. He wouldn't come if anyone could see him. So, everyone stood behind the closed door for a few minutes until my grandmother announced that enough time had passed: Santa had visited their house. They all went back into the living room, and the letters were gone!

When my mother grew up, she asked my grandmother how she'd removed the letters. She said that every year, my grandfather hid behind a large armchair in the corner of the living room. He watched as the children put their letters in the fireplace. As soon as they left the room, he grabbed the letters and then shot back to his hiding spot. He and my grandmother fooled their children for many years.

Fooled their children? Was my grandparents' behaviour deceitful? Dishonest? Or were they weaving a magical fairy tale for the delight of their kids? I wondered about that.

Years ago, I gave up on Santa, not for any deep and meaningful reason, but because I found that keeping up the Santa myth was a lot of work. I didn't have the same dedication as my mother or my grandparents. One day, I heard other parents say that Santa is commercial and we should focus on Christmas' spiritual side. Also, it's wrong to lie to our kids: Santa isn't real. (Although, of course, St Nicholas is.) And I thought these parents had the right ideas. But since then, I've re-examined the Santa issue.

I found these words in an article called *Fairies, Faith and Fantasy* by Fr James Tierney:

The growing realisation as we mature that 'Santa Claus is just your father' is not an exposure of fraud but a cause of even greater joy at the goodwill Providence has shared with man through parents and family life.

Our children find out that we are Santa! We love and care about them enough to bring them the presents they most desire, and we weave magic into their Christmas!

My kids don't have any magical Santa memories, but I do, and so does my mother. Her eyes light up as she tells her childhood Christmas stories. They still bring her joy. And after hearing her tales, our hearts filled with joy, too, at the thought of my grandparents weaving a magical fairy tale that has lasted through the years.

Although Santa has never been part of our family's traditions, we have many other things we enjoy doing together each year.

Here are a few things of our Easter traditions:

- We go to the Easter services together. The Easter Vigil is our favourite Mass. We call it the most beautiful Mass of the year.

- We sing our favourite Easter hymn: *By Your Kingly Power O Risen Lord* on Easter Sunday. For many years, I filmed my family while they were singing. We now have a collection of videos, a different one for each year that we practised this tradition. Watching them, memories of our celebrations flood back. We say such things as, "That was the year Callum left home", "I had braces that year", or "That was before I was born." Unfortunately, one year, I didn't get out my camera, and that was the end of that tradition. I feel sad about that. I guess we could always start it again!

- We light candles.

- Our kids, even though they're older, still like to hunt for eggs. I still enjoy hiding them!

- My husband Andy always cooks a roast lamb feast on Easter Sunday.

- Our girls always bake a chocolate Easter cake. They use shards of chocolate to build a nest on top of the cake and then fill it with little speckled eggs.

- We eat loads of Easter buns.

- I give everyone an Easter parcel containing a few small gifts.

In 2020, we thought we'd miss out on our Easter joy because our churches were closed, and we had other restrictions too. But once we decided to be positive, we found ways to celebrate with joyful hearts.

Some traditions are here to stay forever: we can't imagine life without them. Others are modified or discarded as our children grow. Traditions have to feel right, don't they? If they become a burden, it may be time to do something else.

For many years, my kids placed their shoes in a line on the living room floor on St Nicholas' Eve before going to bed, hoping the saint (or Mum) would come in the night and fill them with gold chocolate coins. Then in 2022, when our youngest daughter was 18, we decided, as a family, to change our St Nicholas tradition. I wanted to wait until Gemma-Rose was an adult before suggesting we leave shoes and coins behind and do something different.

So, after discussing various options, we agreed to bring something golden to a St Nicholas' day feast. Andy provided golden cheeses and biscuits, Gemma-Rose bought sparkling bottles of golden apple cider and wine, and Duncan baked a golden peach pie which went well with Charlotte's golden Hokey Pokey ice cream. Imogen chose everyone a small golden gift, and I handed out gold-wrapped chocolates. We enjoyed our food, and after we'd eaten, we watched a Christmas movie which provided lots for us to discuss!

The Challenge

1. Think about the following questions: What celebrations do you and your children love to do every year? What brings you joy? What traditions do you anticipate repeating over and over again?

2. Are there some traditions you no longer enjoy that you could gently let go of? Could you start some new traditions? Would your kids like to research some ideas with you?

3. You might like to write down your traditions in a special family journal to preserve them forever. You could add some photos. And how about writing out your favourite recipes too?

Traditions bring joy into our lives, but there's another reason why we should cultivate some that are unique to our families. In times of trouble, memories of our traditions might draw our kids back to our family circle. They may remind our children that home is a safe place full of love where they belong.

Of course, when our kids leave home, they might want to create different traditions from the ones they grew up with. This is okay!

Related Reading

You could read my Angel Family children's novels if you'd like to hear more about our traditions and how we celebrate the liturgical year. Mum, Dad and the Angel children seem to enjoy the same traditions as us!

65: Share Childhood Books

My mother saved many of my childhood books, which she returned to me when I got my own home. I was reunited with *The Chalet School*, *The Bobbsey Twins*, *Nancy Drew*, and stories written by Noel Streatfeild and Enid Blyton. Years ago, my books inspired dreams: would I become a ballerina, explorer or an actor? They made me wonder: would boarding school be an enjoyable adventure? And they stimulated my imagination: what would it be like to have a twin sister who looked just like me, someone who'd understand and love me as I was?

When Felicity learnt to read, I remembered the boxes of childhood stories I'd stored in our garage. I unpacked them, eager to share them with my daughter.

Isn't it enjoyable sharing books with other people, especially our kids? There's something extraordinary about having book friends in common. We can talk about the stories, retell our favourite bits, and share what they mean to us.

My kids read all of the old books my mother saved for me, and I read a few of them out loud, including *Ballet Shoes* by Noel Streatfeild. I have so many happy memories of those read-aloud days! I loved revisiting my childhood favourites and seeing my girls' eyes light up as they soaked in the stories. They liked the books as much as me!

As we were reading, I often shared details of my childhood. For example, I told my girls I read *Heidi* while on holiday. While reading in bed, I started crying one night because the story felt so sad. I hoped my mother wouldn't appear because I was embarrassed by my tears. Would she ask, "What's the matter? What are you crying for?" Would I not be able to explain?

Books can lead to all kinds of interesting conversations, can't they? We can learn from them and discover more about each other by sharing them. Shared books can connect us.

The Challenge

1. Make a list of your favourite childhood books.

Do you still have any of them? You might find some of them in a secondhand shop. Many new editions of old books are now available on Amazon.

2. Strew a few.

You could put together a book basket for each of your children. They could dip into them, choosing the ones most appealing to them.

3. Offer to read a book or two out loud.

4. Talk about the books.

Who's your favourite character? Which bit of the book do you like best? Why? Tell stories about the books and your childhood. Soak up the joy of sharing an old book friend.

Don't worry if your childhood favourites don't appeal to your kids. Just enjoy reading them to yourself again!

66: Take Time for Yourself

When my oldest children were young, I often got overtired and overwhelmed with everything I thought I had to do. Life felt like a battle. It wasn't much fun at all.

Sometimes I envied my husband. Andy could leave the house each morning, do paid work others valued, and have adult conversations. I was left behind to do all the work that no one would notice unless I failed to do it. I started to feel resentful about my position in life. I was also angry. This wasn't what I'd imagined life as a mother would be.

Sometimes at the weekend, my husband, sensing that I was unhappy, would say, "What can I do for you? How can I help?" I might have replied, "Could you please finish the dishes? I need a break." Andy would have made me a coffee, and I might have read a book for a few minutes, knowing my husband was cheerfully cleaning the kitchen. But for some strange reason, I always said, "I'm okay." But I wasn't. With a scowl, I dived deeper into the multitude of tasks, not taking time to rest or accept offers of help. I was going to do all the work alone, even if it killed me, which it might have done if I hadn't come to my senses.

There are times when we don't want offers of help. Instead, we want others to notice the chores that must be done and then get on and do them. We want people to read our minds and realise what we need without us saying a word. But that never happens, does it? We just end up miserable as we try not to drown under all the work.

Eventually, I learnt to ask for help which was a great relief for Andy. He could stop trying to guess what he should do to make things better for me. We began working together, so we both got enough rest and opportunities to do something for ourselves.

The other day, after returning from the bush where we'd walked our dogs, I opened our garden gate and said, "Coffee time!" And then I remembered the clean wet washing still in the machine. "I suppose I should hang out the washing first."

Andy said, "You hang the washing, and I'll make the coffee." A feeling of resentment threatened to make an appearance because

Andy had chosen the easier job. I pushed it away, saying, "Please can you help me with the washing? Then we can make the coffee together."

Andy didn't mind this arrangement at all. He grabbed the washing basket, and I got the peg bucket. Our washing was swinging in the breeze a few minutes later: the job was done. And there were no bad feelings because I'd asked for help.

What about you? Do you need help with the chores? With your kids? If you had more free time, what would you do?

We don't have to spend every moment of the day working, do we? Everyone needs opportunities to rest their bodies and minds. So, would you like more time to relax or sleep? Would you lounge in a hammock, doze on a sofa or have a proper nap in bed?

Maybe resting will involve doing something you enjoy. Would you write, play the piano, paint, take photos, cook, renovate that old car waiting for attention or do something else that brings you joy?

Would you like some time to exercise? Working out can be hard to begin, but we always feel good afterwards, don't we?

You could be adventurous and explore by yourself if you can arrange some time away from your family. If you had some alone time, where would you go? What would you do?

How about reading a book? (I read a lot while breastfeeding babies!) You could listen to some music. Or talk on the phone with a friend. Even better, you could meet up with a friend. Arrange to go out for lunch or coffee. It's good to stay strongly connected with the important people who encourage, support and love us. We need trusted friends to share thoughts, ideas, joys and concerns with.

Could you organise some connecting time with your spouse or partner?

How about some pampering? You could soak in a bubble bath, experiment with makeup, pour a glass of wine, apply some body butter, have a manicure, or get a haircut.

Do you find time to pray? As well as benefiting us, our kids need to see us praying and reading our Bibles or doing whatever connects us to our faith or beliefs.

Perhaps you just need to slow down and take time out to savour the simple delights of life:

Enjoy a good cup of coffee.

Sit and look at the view.

Notice your surroundings.

Watch the birds.

Soak up the sunshine.

If you're overtired, why not go with the flow? Don't plough on doing the things you think you should do but have no energy for. Listen to your body.

It's important to look after ourselves, not just for our own happiness but for our kids as well. When we live joyfully instead of resentfully, our joy spreads throughout the family. We don't want to turn into dragon parents, do we?

Also, our kids need to see our example, which shows them it's okay for everyone to rest, exercise and take time out for their interests. We're a family. We're all important, and we must help each other.

The Challenge

1. Think about the things you enjoy doing and list them.

2. Find time for these things by asking for help or ignoring some things that aren't really that important.

3. Slot some of these activities into your day

4. If you have an unexpected quiet moment, consult your list.

You could jot down some notes for a blog post or even a book you'd like to write while taking a short break from your chores. You may have time to read a chapter of a novel while drinking your coffee. Or knit a few rows of your knitting. How about a quick walk around the block or even to the bottom of the garden? Could you read a few verses from your Bible, say a prayer, or sit still and breathe?

5. Keep a book, knitting, notepad, and Bible handy so that you can grab them quickly at opportune moments. You could do the *Strew a Basket* challenge.

6. Do the *Write a Happy List* challenge too!

67: Strew a Lifestyle Show

My family loves watching cooking shows. We watched both series of the British program *The Great Family Cooking Showdown*. Then we discovered *Masterchef* eleven years after it premiered. I don't know why we didn't watch this show sooner. Never mind. We now have hundreds of episodes to enjoy.

Each evening, someone says, "Who wants to watch *Masterchef*?" Everyone does. You could say we're obsessed (not addicted).

Why do we like cooking competitions so much? Is it because we love cooking and want to pick up some new tips and recipes? That might be part of it. But mostly, we love seeing people following their dreams. The contestants are ready to abandon their current jobs to do what they love: cook. That desire speaks to our unschooling hearts.

We also love the creativity of the challenges. It seems there are endless ways to test the skills of the contestants.

Then there's the teamwork and friendships. The episodes of *Masterchef* that we've viewed lack the nastiness that's a part of some other reality shows.

And what about the judging? It's done in an honest but kind and encouraging way.

All my kids can cook. When they were little, they'd join my husband, Andy, in the kitchen. They were his sous-chefs. Andy gave them knives (real ones), and they chopped. Actually, he let them do everything, so they soon gained his cooking skills.

When my daughter Gemma-Rose was sixteen, the cook at the cafe where she worked resigned. The boss interviewed a few applicants for this job vacancy but wasn't happy with any of them. Then he asked Gemma-Rose if she could cook. When he heard she often cooks our family meals and has done this for a long time, he offered her the job of cafe cook. Gemma-Rose accepted, and a few days after she began her new role, I asked, "How are you getting on?

Are you enjoying being the cook?" Gemma-Rose grinned and said, "Yes! It's good. I don't have to wash any dishes!"

It's good to watch a show together, isn't it? It's enjoyable and rewarding sharing our skills, such as cooking, with our kids. And it's wonderful when we can all do the things we love.

The Challenge

1. Find a lifestyle program you think your family might enjoy.

It could be a cooking one. Or how about a renovation program like *Escape to the Castle*, a home decoration show such as *The Great Interior Design Challenge*, or a building-a-unique-home one such as *Grand Designs*? If you don't have any ideas, you could do some googling.

2. Invite your family to watch the show with you.

If no one is interested, watch it anyway. Someone might walk past and say, "What are you watching?" They might linger a moment. They might even sit down and watch the whole episode. If they do, you could end up with a new family obsession!

3. You could challenge yourself to turn your chosen lifestyle program into homeschool records notes.

What did you learn? What school subjects did it cover? Find an image and blurb of the show to add to your notebook. Are there any resources you could strew that might extend both the pleasure and learning experience?

Did you have any conversations while viewing the show? We've had lots of delightful discussions while watching episodes of *Masterchef*.

Kippers

We're watching *Masterchef*. In tonight's episode, there's an identification challenge. Laid out on a table is an array of small, large, speckled, dark, pink, long, flat, thin, goggled-eyed, scaly fish.

The contestants stand in a line waiting for their turn to choose one of the fish and identify it. When someone makes a mistake, a judge says regretfully, "I'm sorry, that's not correct. You're moving into the elimination round." On Sunday, some of the contestants will cook for their lives. Someone will be going home.

Gemma-Rose mutes the TV sound during the ad break, and Imogen asks, "Could you identify any of those fish, Dad?"

"No," says Andy, "I'm not familiar with many fish."

"I can recognise tuna and salmon... if they're in a can," grins Gemma-Rose.

"I know what battered fish looks like," says Charlotte. We like beer-battered fish and chips!

"I can identify kippers," I say

"Kippers?" My girls raise their eyebrows.

"Years ago, Dad and I used to eat kippers for breakfast. They came in plastic bags. They were easy to cook. All we had to do was drop the bags into a pan of boiling water and leave them for a few minutes."

"Were they nice?"

"They must have been because we bought kippers every weekend. That was before we had any children."

Andy and I often tell stories from 'the time before kids'. Our children are fascinated by our past lives, which are, in many ways, very different from theirs.

"What exactly are kippers?" asks Sophie.

"I think they're smoked fish," I reply. "I don't know much else about them."

Imogen takes out her phone and starts googling. Then she says, "'A kipper is a whole herring, a small, oily fish, that has been split in a butterfly fashion from tail to head along the dorsal ridge, gutted, salted or pickled, and cold-smoked over smouldering woodchips. In Britain, Ireland and some regions of North America, kippers are most commonly consumed for breakfast.'"

"Are kippers good for you? Is smoked food good for us?"

More googling. Soon we're going to be kipper experts!

"I wonder if it would be useful to be able to identify lots of different fish," someone says.

"We don't eat much fish."

"Maybe we should. It's good for us."

"It could be fun to know the names of fish."

"If I applied to be a *Masterchef* contestant – which I never will – I'd learn the names of lots of different things: fish, condiments, fruits, herbs, spices...." Sophie says. "I'd be prepared for all kinds of identification challenges."

"Years ago, I wanted to identify different breeds of cattle," I say. "I wanted to know what kinds of cows are in the paddocks between here and town."

Conversations are wonderful, aren't they? We share stories. We ask questions. If we don't know the answers, we google to find out more. We exchange opinions. And because we enjoy discussing things that interest us and are relevant to our lives, we usually remember what we learn.

"Do you remember those cows with the black belts around their middles, the ones that used to be in the fields along the western road? They were Belted Galloways."

"I wonder where those cows went. Do you think their disappearance had anything to do with the drought?"

Our conversation continues. So does *Masterchef*. Somehow we manage to talk and watch at the same time.

Related Reading

Why We Need to Support Our Kids' Choices: Radical Unschool Love

68: Connect with Your Soulmate

I wondered: "Can I arrange a dinner-out picnic for my husband, Andy?"

Sophie was going to town, so I asked her to pick up a couple of gourmet takeaway meals from a favourite cafe. My daughter returned with two portions of chicken tikka curry and rice. I arranged the food on huge white plates. And then I called Andy: "Would you like to join me? We're going out for dinner."

"We are? Where are we going?"

"The front garden. Follow me!"

With the overflowing plates in my hands, I kicked open the front screen door and stepped out into the gorgeous autumn sunshine. Andy grinned when he saw the two rickety chairs and the wobbly wooden table I'd arranged in a secluded spot behind a white flowering shrub. We gingerly took our seats: "Will these old chairs bear our weight?"

"Isn't this wonderful?" I said. "Our own private restaurant."

"Listen to the birds. "

"Can you hear the bees buzzing?"

"Look, a king parrot! He's eating the camellia petals."

My love and I had a perfect dinner-out picnic away from the problems of the world.

Sometimes we need to escape from the world, don't we? Or we might need a break from our everyday concerns. But even if life is running smoothly, we should spend time alone with our spouse or partner to strengthen the bonds between us.

Our relationship with our soulmate is the foundation of our family life. That's the place from which love, respect and trust flow. Our kids need to witness us talking respectfully, listening carefully, considering each other's opinions, making decisions together, being considerate and helpful, forgiving, trusting and loving one another unconditionally. We might already do all this. But are there times when we slip and fail to be good examples of the people we'd like our kids to be? Do we get busy and neglect our relationships?

We may get caught up with our own interests or research (even research about unschooling!). Could we spend too long on social media? We could even spend too much time doing essentially good things, like seeing to the needs of our kids or other people. One day, we might realise that our couple time has shrunk, and we're not talking to each other as much as we used to. Or when we speak, we might not enjoy deep and engaging conversations. We may have drifted our separate ways and no longer do things together. Is it time to tighten the bonds between us?

The Challenge

1. Think about this question: how can I take an interest in my soulmate?

Can you listen more carefully and talk with respect? Are there little things you can do for them? Offer help? Encourage? How about spending more time together? What would you do? Would you go somewhere?

How about asking for your spouse's ideas too? You could go to a cafe to talk about this challenge. Enjoy coffee, hold hands across the table, look in each other's eyes and listen with attention.

2. Make a connecting-together plan.

3. Put it into action!

Andy and I like going out for coffee or lunch for our time together. We connect better when we're engaged in a good conversation that interests both of us while we enjoy our food. Here are a couple of ideas we've used to find new things to chat about:

We like reading the same book. Andy reads a chapter out loud while we enjoy our coffee, and then we discuss it. Usually, we choose a spiritual book, but this idea would work well with a parenting or educational book or even a novel.

We also listen to podcasts. We might choose an episode at the beginning of the week and listen to it separately. We make a few notes of anything we'd like to discuss during our weekend coffee date.

These ideas work well for us because we both like reading and listening. Andy also loves reading out loud. And it's easy for us to fit some podcast listening time into our week. Andy listens while travelling to work, and I listen while walking the dogs.

Another idea: sometimes we search for a news item on our phones that will lead to a conversation. And once, we found a personality quiz online that we each took and then discussed. Phones don't necessarily separate us. They can be used to connect us together.

Discussing books, podcasts and news stories might not appeal to you. But that's okay. There are lots of ways to connect closer as a couple.

Do you enjoy long walks or the same sport? Do you like to share skills as you work on a joint project? What about playing games together? There was a time when Andy and I played chess or backgammon with each other in the evenings. Sadly, we got too competitive. We had to bring our games evenings to an end because they weren't connecting us. They were doing the opposite!

If you have young children, you might think it's too difficult to find some couple time. Doing the things you enjoy the most may seem impossible. But with a bit of creative thinking, you could come up with something you'd both like to do.

When Gemma-Rose was a baby, she had gastric reflux and was very unhappy. Andy and I spent most of our time pacing up and down with her in our arms. But we still managed to get out of the house occasionally. We needed to.

At the end of a difficult day, we'd drive to town, buy a takeaway meal, and then park at the lake to eat it. Sometimes the motion of the moving car would soothe Gemma-Rose to sleep, allowing us to have some quiet time to enjoy our meal. But if she did wake up and cry, we'd take turns holding her while we ate.

We sometimes wondered what would happen if a couple of police officers, hearing our baby's frantic cries, arrived at our car, the only one at the lake. Would they demand to know what we were doing? Making up imaginary conversations amused us. We had fun: we were enjoying an adventure in the dark at the park instead of being stressed at home.

An Extra Challenge

You could write a spouses' happy list as an extension of this challenge. What things do you do together or for each other that make you happy?

Here are a few things Andy and I have on our list that make both of us feel very loved and special :

I often leave inexpensive gifts, usually small items from the supermarket, on Andy's pillow, where he will see them as soon as he comes home from work. These are my pillow presents.

Andy makes me a cup of tea before leaving for work.

Without asking, he fills a glass with wine for me in the evening.

He asks what toiletries and facial products I prefer so he can add them to the grocery list.

He cleans the kitchen before he goes to bed, so I don't have to face any dirty dishes when I get up.

We exchange tiny love note messages when we're apart during the day.

We hold hands when we're out walking.

We have a secret sign that means I love you.

We sometimes enjoy a special dinner at home just for us.

How about you? How will you and your spouse spend time so you can grow close and be safe places for one another and your kids as you navigate the enjoyable but sometimes challenging adventure of your life together?

Related Reading

What if Your Spouse is Reluctant to Unschool?: Curious
Unschoolers

69: Meander the Unschooling Way

There are two routes to our local town. The first one is the efficient way. Once we've left the road that leads out of our village, we drive along the highway through multiple sets of traffic lights before we arrive in town.

The other route is the meandering one that winds through bush and paddocks, round bends, and up hills and down.

If I'm not in a hurry, I like to avoid traffic and go the slower way. I drive past munching cows, lean cyclists treading pedals up the hills, and dams brimming with recent rain. And on the flatter stretches of the road, I let my mind wander: I'm running rhythmically, effortlessly, on the edges of the tarmac, inhaling the wattle-scented air. And as I run, I ponder the different methods of learning.

Perhaps there's a direct way of learning involving an efficient consumption of facts and figures as we work towards a particular goal. Then there's the meandering path with side roads to explore as we ponder, imagine and question. We can crawl up and roll down hills, not worrying about time and where we might end up.

Sometimes as I'm driving the back way to town, a kangaroo or two bounds over a paddock fence and onto the road. With my heart beating fast, I experience an unforgettable closeup, thrilling, dangerous moment of unexpected awe and beauty.

That's the advantage of the meandering route: there's an opportunity for adventurous and unexpected things to happen. There's time for our minds, hearts and souls to engage with whatever comes our way.

There's another reason to leave the road that most people choose: we see a different view of life. We move outside the box. We open ourselves up to possibilities. We question.

We may discover that we prefer to be on the less populated path. It's where exciting things happen.

The Challenge

1. Next time you go somewhere, set out early, and take the longer, less efficient road.

2. Or set off on an adventure with no particular destination in mind. Turn corners randomly. See where you end up.

3. Move your furniture.

4. Change the place where you usually sit in cafes, your living room, church or at your kitchen table. View things from a different angle.

When you slow down and step away from your usual routine, you could notice new things and encounter fresh learning experiences. You may become more open to ideas you never considered before. And will you discover the world is full of delights you failed to recognise because you were always in a hurry?

Will you take time to meander the unschooling way?

70: Ignore People's Opinions

Have you ever put other people ahead of your kids? I have. And I wonder: how could I have done that when my kids mean so much to me? It doesn't make sense, does it?

Years ago, there were many times when I cleaned my house rather than spend time with my children because I wanted my friends, who might drop by unexpectedly, to think I was wonderful. I followed my kids around, picking up their toys as they dropped them. I washed and ironed clothes every day, producing piles of pristine dresses, shirts and t-shirts, not a stain or wrinkle in sight. I wanted my friends to wonder: "How does Sue do it? She has lots of kids and homeschools, and she still finds time to keep such a beautiful home. Why can't I do what Sue does?"

When my kids weren't happy, misbehaved in public or did something else that was potentially embarrassing, I said such things as, "How could you have done that? What will other people think? Never forget you are a reflection of our family." I failed to show empathy and concern: how were my children feeling? Was their behaviour a reflection of an unmet need? What were they dealing with? Did they need my help? I didn't realise that a family should close tightly around a troubled child or parent, providing a safe refuge from the outside world.

I missed opportunities to stand up for my kids, listen to them, and give them what they needed to make them feel loved more than anything else in the world. All I was worried about was impressing other people. I wanted to be accepted, liked, and have a fabulous parent reputation,

Looking back, it seems ironic that while I was trying to maintain my perfect parent image, I wasn't actually a good parent at all. And probably no one liked me that much, either. Pride and perfection aren't very attractive. They don't form connections. Unless, of course, our friends have similar outlooks to us, sharing our ambitions. And even then, competitiveness can obliterate real friendship.

Why are we so anxious to be liked and accepted? Why don't we have enough confidence to go our own way and do what we feel is right? Why do we worry about what other people think of us? Are we all trying to fill holes deep within us, created during our own upbringings, the result of not being accepted for the people we are? Perhaps we need reassurance that we're okay.

Imagine what would happen if we refused to do things only to please other people but instead listened to our kids. Would our children grow up feeling secure, loved, accepted for themselves, and confident? Would they, unlike us, not feel the need to model themselves on the opinions of others but be themselves, regardless of the consequences? Would they feel at peace?

Years ago, I parted ways with the friends I was anxious to impress. I'm no longer important to them. Probably they don't even remember me.

But, unlike those mothers, my kids are still here. And I now put them first and don't worry what others think of us. I've learnt to look at the love in my children's eyes to get a true picture of what parenting is all about rather than searching for answers elsewhere. As a family, we do what we feel is right, regardless of everyone's opinions.

Do you do that too? Or are you struggling not to look for acceptance? If you'd like to explore this issue, you may want to do this challenge.

The Challenge

1. Find a pen and paper or open your device.

2. Set a timer for ten minutes.

3. Free write about opinions, expectations, kids, and other people, pouring your thoughts onto the page or screen without stopping.

Here are some questions you could explore:

Why do we worry about what others think of us? Are their opinions worth listening to?

Do we do things to be accepted and liked? Do we follow the crowd so they'll accept our kids and want to be friends? Is acceptance good? Can it encourage us to do what is right? But are there times when we end up doing things that aren't good for our kids?

Why do we need acceptance? Do we lack confidence? Did we not feel good enough while we were growing up? Are we searching for a place to belong?

Do we listen to our kids to discover their needs? Or do we listen to our friends and family?

Who are the most important people in our lives? Who do we hope will be part of our lives forever? Our friends that we're eager to impress? Or our kids?

It doesn't matter where you start. You just need to write and not stop until your time is up.

4. Read what you've written. You may discover an idea or thought that's worth exploring in more depth. If you do, free write about it for another ten minutes.

Would we embrace unschooling without hesitation if we weren't concerned about the negative comments others might say or even think? "Are you crazy? Are you irresponsible?"

Would we accept our kids exactly as they are if we weren't so eager to look like good parents in the eyes of our friends and family? "Don't do that! What will people think?"

Would we be happier if we were more confident and did what we felt was right instead of worrying about being accepted by a group of people who are also desperate to be accepted? And would our kids be happier too?

Years ago, I didn't want our new friends to find out about our heavy metal music collection. What would they think of us if they saw our records? I persuaded my husband to remove his treasured vinyl albums from our lives before they were discovered.

The Heavy Metal Music Removal

Every birthday, Andy buys Gemma-Rose a heavy metal t-shirt. Our daughter knows nothing about this kind of music except it was a big part of her dad's life when he was her age. And that makes it special to her.

When Andy and I were young parents, we invited new friends to lunch, and while I was giving them a tour of our home, I noticed how they raised their eyebrows when they saw my huge Stephen King book collection. Although they didn't say anything directly, the conversation turned towards the subject of keeping our kids safe from the bad influences in the world: books, TV shows, and music. We have to be careful what we allow into our homes. My books were obviously on the unapproved list. What about our heavy metal music collection? I knew I had to get rid of it fast before our new friends discovered it and realised we were irresponsible parents, unlike them.

So Andy reluctantly hauled all his treasured music records and all my books to the tip. I felt sad. Years of our lives were being tossed away into the garbage. But I was also relieved. We'd created a safe home. We could invite people over without worrying about what they'd think of us. Maybe we'd be regarded as good, caring parents and be liked and accepted.

Is heavy metal music dangerous? Should we not read Stephen King books? Did our friends save our kids and us from bad influences? Maybe. Maybe not. That's not the point of this story.

What I'm thinking about is this:

Often we make decisions based on the opinions and expectations of others. Without considering whether something is good for us or not, whether it suits our family or fulfils our needs and those of our children, we toss away anything that might make us unacceptable in the eyes of other people. All it takes is a few words, the tone of someone's voice, or some raised eyebrows, and we begin to doubt ourselves.

Why don't we stand firm and have confidence in our opinions and decisions? Why don't we trust ourselves? Why are we so easily swayed by other people? Is it because we have a deep longing for acceptance and a place to belong?

Gemma-Rose wears her Metallica t-shirt, which doesn't indicate a love of heavy metal music. Instead, it represents a connection between a father and a daughter. It's a symbol of their love.

Love?

Are strong bonds of love and connection the best way to keep our kids safe?

Pleasing Our Friends Instead of God

Do you ever worry about what people think of you? Do you need others to approve of you? Perhaps, like me, you've wanted your family and friends to tell you you're doing an excellent job with your kids.

There may be nothing wrong with receiving pats on the backs from those around us. It's encouraging, isn't it? But what if we receive praise and approval, but we're not doing what God wants us to do?

Do we sometimes know, deep in our hearts, what we should be doing but fail to do it because it would mean standing alone? People might criticise us. Praise feels so much better! Maybe we don't want to admit that we'd rather put the approval of others ahead of our kids and God's will for our families.

Our friends and family don't know what's best for our kids, but we often let them dictate what we do. I regret following the crowd to gain approval. It affected my relationship with my kids because I failed to help them with their needs.

Following the crowd also affects our relationship with God.

Do we put others ahead of God when we fail to do what we know is right for our families? Do we care more about how people view us than pleasing God?

I guess the big question is: do we believe God wants us to unschool? Is this the right thing to do?

Related Reading

Fingerprints of Love: Radical Unschool Love

71: Be Heroic

Usually, I get up earlier than my husband Andy, but recently I wasn't feeling well, so I lingered in bed. By the time I got up, Andy, our bedmaker, had left for work, and I had to do this task.

That evening, I thanked Andy for always pulling the sheets tight and straightening the quilt on our bed. For years, he's done this job without complaining. Actually, Andy does a lot of things around our house that make a difference. And our kids have noticed.

Parents often talk about chores: how do we encourage our kids to do them? We want our children to be responsible and helpful people. How do we do that? Sometimes parents put together chore charts to ensure kids do their fair share of work. But even if chore charts worked, is being fair enough? Being generous people who don't count the cost is even better.

Encouraging our kids to be generous people isn't easy. We can't just tell them what they should do and how we want them to be. Instead, we need to forget what's fair and do more than expected ourselves. Be an example of generosity for our kids.

Sometimes the experts warn parents not to let kids take advantage of them: "Don't do too much for your kids. Make them look after themselves." But if we hold back and refuse to help, will our kids become self-focused? They may not look beyond themselves and want to do more than the minimum.

Generosity often involves a heroic effort. But when we don't feel like doing something and push ourselves to do it anyway, we encourage each other to go beyond the expected, to be generous and do more than fairness demands.

And if we can't be generous because we're overtired or unwell, our family will quickly say, "I'll do that for you! Go and rest!"

We help our kids, and they help us. Heroic effort is all about love.

And I love Andy and our smoothly-made bed.

The Challenge

1. Look out for opportunities to be heroic.

When you're tired and only want to see to yourself, consider whether other people are tired too. Can you dig deep and do what's needed?

2. Forget about the word 'fair'. Don't keep a balance sheet.

3. Refuse to worry about spoiling your kids.

4. Love until it hurts.

And if you're exhausted or sick and unable to give, accept your family's help and soak up their love. They'll step into the breach and follow your example.

Related Reading

A Generous Attitude: Radical Unschool Love

Fairness: Radical Unschool Love

72: Replace Charlotte Mason

Do some aspects of the various methods of homeschooling appeal to you? How about living books? And art and nature studies? What about the classics? Journaling and drawing?

Years ago, Charlotte Mason's ideas drew me in. There's something very attractive about her way of doing things, isn't there?

Short lessons make sense for kids who can't sit still. And shouldn't children spend lots of time outside playing and exploring nature? And I understand why narration is required. It gives kids the opportunity to make any knowledge their own. Also, it's good to appreciate art that tells a story or engages our emotions and senses. Then there's music that sings to our souls and living books that capture our imaginations. And shouldn't we be filling our heads with noble ideas?

Our hearts might be captivated by Charlotte Mason. Is that because this method of homeschooling is based on all that's beautiful, good and true?

Despite many attempts, we never managed to successfully 'do' Charlotte Mason. Although all would go well for a time, eventually, my kids protested: "Why do we have to do this?" and I replied, "Because it's in my lesson plan. Because I said so." What I really meant was, "Because Charlotte Mason says so." My kids and I would start to battle. Unfortunately, this wasn't beautiful, good and true.

As you might know, one day, I abandoned my search for the perfect method of homeschooling. I stopped trying to force other people's ideas onto my children and began listening to them instead. I trusted that they could learn without imposing an external method on them. So I said goodbye to Charlotte Mason forever. However, I had a few regrets because all those promises of goodness, truth and beauty still attracted my heart.

Maybe you feel the same. Your mind could tell you that unschooling makes sense and is the right thing to do. But your heart is not so sure. It keeps looking over its shoulder at Charlotte Mason, wanting what it feels it needs.

One day, I realised that even though I'd rejected Charlotte Mason, I hadn't turned my back on beauty, truth and goodness. Living books, beautiful paintings, nature, poetry, Shakespeare, and noble ideas aren't the exclusive property of a particular homeschooling method. They are part of our fascinating world. Our kids can come into contact with them just by living life. And if there's anything, in particular, we'd like our kids to be aware of, we can always strew it.

We could hang a painting on the wall, invite our kids to explore nature with us, offer to read some living books to them, invite them to watch a Shakespeare play with us, strew a poem, say, "I've been thinking about..." and share some thoughts and ideas.

Of course, we can't force our strewing on our kids. So yes, they may reject our invitations. But I've discovered that my kids, being curious people, often get caught up in my enthusiasm and are very open to my strewing suggestions.

It might seem better to surround our kids with beauty, truth and goodness the Charlotte Mason way because kids can't reject what we'd like them to learn about. Of course, they might like what's in the plan. Then again, they might not. But it seems to me it's better if kids have a choice. Then when they do choose to read a poem, listen to a book, or look at a painting, they'll be fully engaged. Their hearts will be wide open, ready to absorb all that beauty, truth and goodness.

The triple treasures we yearn for abound in unexpected places. We don't have to stick only to the classical. Good isn't always old. (And old isn't always good!) It took me a while to realise this. Years ago, when I was in one of my Charlotte Mason phases. I searched high and low for copies of all the old books that Charlotte Mason used. I remember how excited I got whenever I did manage to track one down. (Old books were harder to find in those pre-Internet days.) But those books weren't necessary. Goodness, truth and beauty can be found in today's world as well as in times gone by.

Someone once said to me, "The classical period of music was the greatest. No composer or musician will ever be as good as those of that era."

If that were true, wouldn't it be sad?

The Challenge

1. Enrich your home with beauty, truth and goodness.

Hang paintings and prints on the walls. Play music that sings to your soul. Stock your bookshelves with living books. You could buy or hire a piano or keyboard or another instrument. Display photos and ornaments that you love. Arrange flowers in vases. Drape soft, snuggly throws on your chairs and toss cushions on your sofa. Place a few spiritual books where everyone can see and use them.

2. Strew more beauty, truth and goodness.

Say such things as "I'm going to watch *Swan Lake.* Does anyone want to join me?" Add links to plays, poems, paintings, novels, art history videos and music to your strewing notebook. Offer to read living books. Strew a few blank journals in case your kids want to fill them with words or drawings.

3. Recognise the beauty, truth and goodness that your kids are already experiencing.

Did you know there are lots of these in many video games? What could be more beautiful than the desire to set out on a mission to protect the good, build up your virtues and use your talents to fight evil?

4. Find beauty, truth and goodness in the bigger world.

Suggest outings to museums, art galleries, open and botanic gardens, parks, the beach, the bush, or a lake.

5. If you can't travel the world, take a virtual tour.

Visit ancient castles, awe-inspiring churches, national parks and wild, rugged places online.

6. Forget about short lessons.

They're not needed. Kids are good at concentrating. Just watch small children looking at worms, leaves, caterpillars, shadows or even drops of water. They are captivated and absorbed. It's adults who want to rush past all the fascinating things. We're the ones in a hurry. We don't seem to have the same patience as our kids.

If kids do have a problem sitting still, could the lessons be the problem rather than them? Are traditional methods of teaching failing to capture a child's attention? Are they foreign to a child's natural way of learning? Or are kids not ready for the information? Could it not be what they need at the moment?

7. Forget about narration.

We don't need to force a child to retell what they've just heard or write it down. All we have to do is listen. Most kids are eager to talk about the things that fascinate or excite them. Adults like to do this too. I often say, "Guess what I just heard... Can I tell you about...? Wow, this is so interesting!" Narration isn't necessary if we're in the habit of listening to our kids with our full attention.

If we make beauty, truth and goodness an integral part of our family lives, we won't have to turn to Charlotte Mason. Our kids will absorb these foundational things with open hearts without her help. We can stop looking over our shoulders and embrace unschooling fully, knowing it will provide everything our souls desire.

73: Play the Educational Language Game

Not so long ago, we saw small white butterflies everywhere. They flittered amongst the flowers in our garden; they flew through the park; they chased each other across the motorway that leads towards town.

"Have you noticed all the butterflies?" I asked my husband, Andy. "There seem to be more of them than usual. Do you think that's because of the abundant rain? And what kind of butterflies are they?"

Andy gave me his opinion, and after a bit of googling, we confirmed that the butterflies were cabbage white butterflies and, yes, their prolific numbers were due to the unusually wet weather. The butterflies are pretty, but are their larvae considered a pest? Did the larger-than-normal numbers devastate gardens and crops? Another question. More research as we searched for answers.

"What's the proper name for a group of butterflies?" I asked, and Andy suggested it's 'flutter'. Google agreed with my husband, but we discovered that this isn't the only correct collective noun. Flights, rabbles and kaleidoscopes of butterflies have also been flying through our village.

"It's interesting how there are multiple collective nouns for some animals," I said. "Different people must have proposed different words. We could make up our own noun too." After a moment's thought, I said, "Normally, we talk about flocks of sheep, but we could call a group of unshorn sheep a 'sweater of sheep'. And then once the shearers have deprived them of their wool, they could be called a 'shiver of sheep'." Andy and I giggled as we imagined a field of skinny cold sheep. I bet shorn sheep don't giggle.

Although our registered homeschooling days are behind us, I still wonder how I could translate our enjoyable butterfly and sheep conversation into the correct educational language for a record-keeping notebook. Here are a few ideas:

Butterflies are science. We identified the butterflies. We asked questions, proposed answers and researched butterflies online. We looked at images and read descriptions. We read about the butterfly's lifecycle and discovered what plants the cabbage white butterfly likes to eat.

As well as science, we did lots of English. We'd remembered that a word describing a group of nouns is a collective noun. As well as researching collective nouns, we created our own and used them in some sentences. I even wrote them down so I remember them. I want to use them in a blog post or story. That's creative writing. We also researched a few other collective nouns: a group of caterpillars is called an army.

We did our research using our phones. That's technology.

If we'd got out our records notebook, we might have added:

- Copies of the online articles we read.

- Images of the cabbage white butterflies - I took photos of them rabbling around our garden flowers.

- And copies of my amazingly creative collective nouns and sample sentences.

So Andy and I did science, English and technology without even meaning to. As far as we were concerned, we were just enjoying a fun conversation.

That's the point, isn't it? We're learning all the time, whether we realise it or not. Learning is woven naturally into our lives, and sometimes we don't even notice it. But if we become better at spotting it, we'll have no shortage of learning experiences to add to our homeschool record-keeping notebooks. With practice, when we see our kids engaged in an activity, we will instantly think 'science', 'technology' or 'English' without a problem.

Is it wrong to dissect everything our kids are involved with as we look for the appropriate educational language? It might seem sad to describe our amazing lives as maths, science or creative arts. Those labels don't convey the richness of unschooling, do they? They might make unschooling look rather ordinary.

Yes, unschooling isn't meant to be described using schooly-type words. We can't really reduce it to a list of outcomes. So why try to put an unstructured unschooling life into an organised framework? Unfortunately, like many families, we needed to keep records of our kids' learning for registration purposes. And those records had to correspond with the school syllabus. From my notes, our Authorised Person (AP) could see my kids were learning. Maybe she suspected our records didn't tell the whole story: our unschooling life was much richer than they suggested!

So, we may have to think about record keeping if our kids are registered homeschoolers because we need evidence that our kids are learning the school subjects. We have to turn unschooling into the correct educational language.

The Challenge

1. Choose a conversation or activity that involved your kids.

2. Write down what you talked about and what you did. Go slowly, step by step, and list all the details.

So many times, we sum up everything too quickly. We might say, "We went shopping." That was it. There's not much we can add.

But what did we buy? Did we get any bargains? Did we compare prices?

Did we look at the cost per unit to find the best buy? Did we see any percentage-off signs or special 3 for the price of 2 offers? Did we work out how much money we'd save? We could have talked about budgets, not wasting money, and vegetables and fruits that were in season.

Did we look at volumes, weights and sizes? Did we talk about how much of each item we needed? Perhaps we consulted a recipe? Did we look at use-by dates? Did we read any food packaging labels? Maybe we took our own reusable shopping bags? Or did we buy plastic ones? Did we assess the success of the elimination of one-use bags?

How did we pay for our shopping? Cash or card? Credit or debit? Did we swipe our rewards card? How many reward points did we gain? Did we use the self-serve checkout or one with an assistant?

We probably talked about all kinds of things while walking up and down the supermarket aisles. Did the checkout assistant chat with us too?

3. Watch out for educational words such as 'question', 'propose', 'compare', 'research', 'read', 'count', 'date', and "discuss".

4. List any equipment and skills you used.

5. Label all the details of your learning experience with the appropriate school subjects.

6. Add some photos of everything you and your children experienced.

Deciding on the correct educational language might seem difficult at first. However, it gets easier with practice. You could regard it as a game. Challenge yourself to find as many learning experiences and subject labels as quickly as possible. Soon it will become second nature.

One day, while discussing butterflies with your spouse, you just might find the words 'science' and 'English' and 'technology' appearing automatically in your mind!

74: Discover Some Christmas Maths

Here in Australia, our official school year ends in December, so towards the end of November, many homeschoolers start saying, "When are you finishing up for the year?" Will everyone last until the end of the term? Perhaps some people will announce, "That's it! I've had enough. Let's begin the holidays early!"

As unschoolers, our family never 'finished up' for the year because learning never stops, does it? It just looks different depending on where we are in the year.

One year, as Christmas approached, I knew my kids were still learning all kinds of things while we were spending our time shopping, wrapping gifts, and getting involved with the liturgical activities we enjoy during the Advent season, but I wondered: were they using their maths skills? Is there much maths hidden amongst all the Christmas festivities?

I decided to become a Christmas maths detective and discovered loads of it! While you're busy buying gifts, decorating your home, watching festive movies and talking about how you're going to celebrate the Christmas season, you could search for maths too.

The Challenge

1. Put on your maths eyes!

Do you have an Advent calendar with numbers on it? Are you counting down the days to Christmas?

Are you cooking gingerbread, mince pies and other Christmas goodies? There's lots of maths inside a recipe.

What about shopping? Do you have a spending budget? An upper money limit for gifts? Have you bought anything in a sale, 50% off? Are your children buying their own gifts? Are you and your children browsing number-filled gift catalogues?

How many Christmas cards have you received? Only a few? How many did you send? How much does a Christmas card stamp cost?

2. Listen.

Have you had any Christmas conversations with your family? Perhaps you've been curious people and asked lots of questions. Here are a few that my family has pondered:

What are the most popular Christmas movies? When were they made? How much money did they make at the box office? What Tomatometer rating do they have?

Are real trees more popular than artificial ones? Does the answer depend on the country? How long does it take to grow a perfect Christmas tree? When did people start decorating trees? When was the first artificial tree produced for sale? On average, how long does a fake tree last?

When did people start giving each other Christmas cards? How many are sent every year? Are real cards more popular than e-cards?

What countries celebrate Christmas during the winter? And which ones have a summer Christmas?

I'm sure you can think of many more questions.

3. Enjoy researching the questions and discussing the answers!

When my family gathers together, and I ask a Christmas question, someone grabs their phone to find out the answer, and then we have a fantastic conversation. Maybe the same thing will happen in your home.

There are some fabulous Christmas infographics that contain lots of numbers. While you're googling, you might discover some. I found one about the 12 days of Christmas. How much would it cost your true love to buy you all the gifts in the song?

4. If you have to keep homeschooling records:

- Take photos of your Advent calendar and your Christmas recipes and baking.

- Jot down the details of your Christmas conversations.

- Add links to any articles you read. Or copy and paste them.

- Find some Christmas movie and book cover images.

- And if you find any good Christmas infographics that involve maths, add them to your notebook too.

- Label your notes 'maths' or 'math'.

- And add relevant tags such as 'cardinal numbers', 'ordinal numbers', 'money', 'counting', 'measurement', 'percentages', 'seasons', 'calendar', 'dates', 'profit', 'addition', 'subtraction', 'average', 'comparison'.

You may be surprised by how much maths we use during the Advent and Christmas seasons. Although we might not be thinking about learning, it's still happening!

Extra Challenges

Of course, you can repeat this challenge at other times of the year, including Easter.

75: Write an End-of-the-Year Review

The changeover of the years is an excellent time to examine our lives, isn't it? As Socrates said, *An unexamined life is not worth living.* Yes, we should think about the year that's just ended. What did we learn? How did we grow? Is our family going in the right direction? Do we need to make some changes? And what will we take forward with us into the year that's about to begin? What are our hopes?

We may have had a tough year, and we could be reluctant to examine the difficulties we faced. Maybe we just want to forget them and move on, saying, "I hope next year will be better!"

2020 was a tough year, wasn't it? The first word that comes to mind when I think about it is 'awful'. We lost our freedom and endured a lockdown. My husband and children either lost their jobs or had to work from home because of covid restrictions. I was lonely. "I hope it's all over by Christmas," I said. But it wasn't. With another lockdown and vaccine mandates, 2021 was worse than 2020. But it wasn't all bad, which was just as well because we can't ignore a year or two of our lives and pretend they didn't happen, can we?

Each year is important. Good or bad, each one represents 365 days of our kids' lives and ours as well. Would we really wish a year away and do without that time with our family? Every moment we have together is precious.

The Challenge

1. Make a cup of coffee or tea, settle down with your journal, ready to review your year. Or gather together as a family to talk about the last twelve months. Or do both!

2. Think carefully about your year. Don't take it at face value. Look between the obviously good bits for the positives hidden amongst the difficult days.

Here are some questions you could ponder:

- Did you have any magical moments with your kids?

- How did your kids grow and develop and delight you?

- Did you face any difficult times as a family? Did they bind you closer together?

- Did you explore anything new this year?

- Did you take another step along the unschooling path? Were you able to let go of anything that used to worry you?

- Did you change in any way? Did your kids?

- What enjoyable things did you do with your family? What made you laugh? What touched your hearts?

This challenge could have a rule: choose to be positive.

It would be so easy to get bogged down in the negatives, wouldn't it? But it would be sad if our difficulties affected our joys. If you'd like to list your concerns, including any worries about your kids, can you turn them around until you find something positive to take their place?

I'll never forget the difficulties of our covid-affected years, but I will also remember the good things buried amongst the frustrations and fears. Here are just a few of the positives:

We got to spend extra time together as a family.

My husband learnt new skills as he adapted to online learning.

I conquered my fear of Zoom, which opened up new possibilities.

We learnt a lot about viruses and how they work!

We thought deeply about the meaning of freedom.

So, was your unschooling year good? Did you have no trouble finding delights and achievements to add to your journal or your family conversation? Or did you have to go deeper until you could see that the year you experienced with your family was okay?

Wouldn't it be good to end every year, not just the easy ones, feeling grateful for what we've experienced? Instead of wanting to forget the year completely, turning our backs on it with relief, we could compile a list of joyful memories and encouraging moments that will propel us into January with enthusiasm for another unschooling year with our families.

We should be thankful for every year, shouldn't we? Easy or difficult, they all happen for a reason.

76: Be Brave

The title of Robin Sharma's book *The 5 am Club* caught my eye because I'm always up at that hour of the day. I wondered: do I already belong to this club?

I started reading and discovered that club members start their day with 20 minutes of cardio exercise. I gulped. Surely no one rolls out of bed early and immediately starts moving at a heart-racing pace? And then I remembered that's exactly what my girls and I did for many years. We'd pull on our shorts, t-shirts and shoes and head out the door as the sun was rising. Then we'd run along the bush tracks before coming home for breakfast.

We were The Team. We were strong. We looked difficulties in the face and laughed.

The Team broke up when my girls, one by one, started work and lost their early morning freedom. For a while, I ran by myself. Then one morning, when the weather was cold and extra miserable, I didn't run. I convinced myself that running in the winter was a stupid idea. I didn't have to do it. I was an unschooler in charge of my own life. I was free to do what I liked.

Months went by. I regularly did cardio workouts in the comfort of my home at a sensible hour of the day, but I didn't run along the bush tracks.

Then one day, I got up at 5 am as usual, but instead of making some tea and grabbing my iPad to check the mail, I pulled on my exercise clothes. Bleary-eyed, I did a short cardio workout while waiting for the sky to lighten, and then I laced up my shoes and ran down to the bush.

The air was refreshingly cool, the brilliant bushfire orange sun was rising between the gum trees, and I could hear nothing except the birds singing. I realised that I'd been missing the best part of the day. I ran, not 5 km like I used to, but a reasonable distance, and came home grinning. I'd run, my feet dancing over the rocks with the breeze lifting my hair. I wanted to do it again. And again. I yearned to be strong and gritty. I wanted to look challenges in the face and laugh.

I started writing this book a long time ago. It was an exciting project at first. But then the excitement disappeared, and all I could see was work and more work. Questioning whether I wanted to finish the book, I put the manuscript aside for a while and did easy things such as aimlessly browsing the Internet. But I soon discovered that avoiding the hard work of writing didn't make me happy. I knew God created me for more than easy endless scrolling. It was time for me to be brave and face the difficult things: I challenged myself to get up at 5 am, run, and also finish *The Unschool Challenge.*

How about you? Do you yearn to do something worthwhile too? Do you want to feel the satisfaction that results from conquering challenges? Would you like your kids to follow your example and use their freedom to work hard on the things that matter to them?

Do you want to feel brave enough to do what you think is right for your kids even if it's difficult?

Even when we know what we should do, it can be hard to actually do it, can't it? Excuses rush in to divert our attention away from our chosen goal. We tell ourselves we're too busy, too old, or too tired. We haven't got enough experience, it's too late or our talents aren't needed. Sometimes the most difficult thing about doing something difficult is silencing those voices so we can begin.

The Challenge

1. Be brave:

- Choose something that you'd like to do but haven't yet done because it seems too difficult.

- Embrace a challenge that comes your way without an invitation.

- Do what is right even if this causes difficulties for you.

- View the tough times of parenting with eyes of love and keep moving forward, knowing you are making a difference.

2. Enjoy the fruits of being brave and gritty. Other people might benefit from your efforts too.

Here's one last story before I finish this book:

One evening, Andy asked, "What time are you running in the morning?" When I replied, "5:30," my husband said, "Wake me up, and I'll come with you."

So, the next day, just after sunrise, we both ran laps of the playing field next to the bush close to our home. It was like the 'old days' when Andy, our girls and I used to run together. Most mornings, we'd roll out of bed early and work hard running along the bush tracks or around the field. Then we'd high-five each other, and I'd say, "Good work, Team!" before we walked home for breakfast.

On the same day that Andy and I ran together, I went out for coffee with my youngest daughter. As we sipped our lattes, we chatted about all kinds of things before Gemma-Rose said, "I need your advice, Mum. I'm thinking about joining a gym. If I had a membership, I could do strength training and run on the treadmill after work. What do you think?" We then talked about running, exercise gear, and training for fun runs. It was just like the 'old days'.

Sometimes stages of our lives end as our kids grow older and move on to new things. We might feel sad and wish we could go back in time. But those special days don't disappear without a trace. Everyone takes something from them as we all move forward: the memories, the close connections, the values we shared, the lessons we learnt. These are inside us, part of who we are today.

It's unlikely we'll ever run again as a family. We no longer have the freedom to do that. But our early morning running days are still with us. They gave us the desire to be fit and strong. They taught us not to fear difficult things but to welcome challenges. They bonded us together.

So I'm running each morning, and it looks like Andy wants to run with me. And Gemma-Rose is joining a gym so she can run too. (I also heard Sophie is now training for a half-marathon.) I wonder what else will happen because, one day, I laced up my running shoes and headed out the door, searching for a challenge.

It's never just about us, is it? What we choose to do affects those around us. Our example is very important. It could lead to experiences that will stay with us all forever.

I hope *The Unschool Challenge* isn't just about me. I'd love the hard work contained in this book to ripple out into the world. Maybe the challenges will encourage you to be brave and do something that might at first feel difficult: step deeper into unschooling.

Please let me know - and others too - if my book makes a difference to you.

Now that I've finished *The Unschool Challenge*, the big question is: what's next? Is it time for me to sit back, focus on myself and enjoy life. I could spend my days reading, walking dogs, knitting, watching YouTube and drinking coffee. One of my kids suggested that after many years of parenting, homeschooling and sharing unschooling with others, it would be quite okay to do this: "You've done your work, Mum. It's time to take time for yourself." Yes, I could take life easy.

But I don't think I'm finished yet. I'm sure there are still big things ahead of me. New adventures to enjoy, lots of challenges to embrace and more learning to do.

And more love.

Love is what's most important, isn't it? Love helps us to be brave and do what is right. It helps us to meet challenges and do difficult things. It's the reason we get up in the middle of the night to comfort a child when we'd rather stay in bed.

Love is at the heart of our unschooling lives.

And this is the very last thought I'd like to leave with you:

When in doubt, when you don't know what to do, choose love.

Related Reading

Be Brave: Radical Unschool Love

Because I Am a Mother: Radical Unschool Love

Where You Can Find Me

Online

Blog: Stories of an Unschooling Family

Podcast: Stories of an Unschooling Family

YouTube channel: Sue Elvis

Instagram: stories_ofan_unschoolingfamily

My Unschooling Books

Curious Unschoolers

Radical Unschool Love

My Children's Novels

The Angels of Abbey Creek

The Angels of Gum Tree Road

The Angels of Wallaby Way

Acknowledgements

Thank you to my daughter Imogen for proofreading and formatting this book. And thank you to my daughter Charlotte for creating its fabulous cover.

And a huge thank you to my brilliant family Andy, Felicity, Duncan, Callum, Imogen, Charlotte, Thomas, Sophie and Gemma-Rose for letting me write your stories. Without you, there would be no book.

About the Author

Sue Elvis is a long time unschooling mother who lives with her husband Andy and some of their eight children somewhere south of Sydney, Australia.

Sue spends a lot of time walking or running through the beautiful Australian bush with her family and dogs, Nora and Quinn. She also loves heading out on solo adventures with her camera in hand.

When Sue isn't busy sharing the unschooling message via her books, Youtube channel, podcast and blog, she enjoys adding a dash of imagination to the stories of her family's life, turning them into fiction for children.

Made in United States
Troutdale, OR
09/06/2023

12694182R00170